PETER OF JOHN OLIVI

COMMENTARY ON THE GOSPEL
OF MARK

TRANSLATION, INTRODUCTION, AND NOTES BY
ROBERT J. KARRIS, O.F.M.

© Franciscan Institute Publications

Published 2011 by
St. Bonaventure University
Saint Bonaventure, NY 14778

Franciscan Institute Publications would like to thank
the University of Glasgow Library, Department of Special Collections, for
its permission to use the image of St. Mark,
image of folio 110v, MS Hunter 475, on the cover.
Cover design by Emily Hurlburt

ISBN 13: 978-1-57659-234-2
ISBN 10: 1-57659-234-0

Library of Congress Cataloging-in-Publication Data

Olivi, Pierre Jean, 1248 or 9-1298.
    [Lectura super Marcum. English]
    Commentary on the Gospel of Mark / Peter of John Olivi ; trans-
lation, introduction, and notes by Robert J. Karris.
        p. cm.
    Includes bibliographical references and indexes.
    ISBN 978-1-57659-234-2 (alk. paper)
    1. Bible. N.T.--Commentaries--Early works to 1800. I. Karris,
Robert J. II. Title.
    BS2585.53.03913 2011
    226.3 ' 0709022--dc22

                                                    2011013904

Printed in the United States of America
BookMasters, Inc.
Ashland, Ohio

TABLE OF CONTENTS

ABBREVIATIONS

CCSL	Corpus Christianorum. Series Latina.
CSEL	Corpus Scriptorum Ecclesiasticorum Latinorum
Glossa	Glossa ordinaria
NAB	*New American Bible*, Catholic World Press, 1990; World Bible Publishers.
NPNF	Nicene and Post-Nicene Fathers. Grand Rapids: Eerdmans.
NRSV	*New Revised Standard Version: Catholic Edition* (Nashville: Catholic Bible Press, 1993)
PL	Patrologiae Cursus Completus. Series Latina. Ed. J.P. Migne.
WAE	The Works of Aristotle. Volumes 1-12. Translated into English under the Editorship of W. D. Ross. London: Oxford University Press, 1928.
WSB	Works of Saint Bonaventure

Old Testament

Gen	1 Chron	Wis	Obadiah
Ex	2 Chron	Sir	Jonah
Lev	Ezra	Isa	Micah
Num	Nehemiah	Jer	Nah
Deut	Tob	Lam	Hab
Joshua	Judith	Bar	Zeph
Judges	Esther	Ez	Haggai
Ruth	Job	Dan	Zech
1 Sam	Ps	Hosea	Mal
2 Sam	Prov	Joel	1 Macc
1 Kings	Qoh	Amos	2 Macc
2 Kings	Cant		

New Testament

Matt	1 Cor	1 Thes	James
Mark	2 Cor	2 Thes	1 Peter
Luke	Gal	1 Tim	2 Peter
John	Eph	2 Tim	1 John
Acts	Phil	Titus	2 John
Rom	Col	Phlm	3 John
		Hebr	Jude
			Rev

INTRODUCTION

OLIVI AS A BIBLICAL EXEGETE

Franciscan friar Peter of John Olivi (1248-1298) was educated in Paris and lectured for most of his academic life in Franciscan study houses (*studia*), especially in the south of France.[1] Olivi's *Commentary on the Gospel of Mark* bears the title, *Lectura super Marcum*, and no doubt stems from his lectures in a Franciscan study house. I will briefly discuss his other biblical lectures, so that readers might better understand in what ways Olivi's *Commentary on the Gospel of Mark* is unique and at the same similar to his other biblical lectures.

---

[1] It is not my intention to enter into more details of Peter of John Olivi's life and thought. Nor do I intend to rehearse how his Franciscan Order and the papacy responded to his thought. Nor is it my intention to explore the fact that thousands of people from all over Languedoc participated in the popular, but ecclesiastically unsanctioned celebration of the "feast" of Peter of John Olivi at his tomb in the Franciscan church at Narbonne. For general orientation to many aspects of the life and thought of Peter of John Olivi, see *Pierre de Jean Olivi (1248-1298): Pensée scolastique, dissidence spirituelle et société*, edited by Alain Boureau and Sylvain Piron, Études de philosophie médiévale 79 (Paris: J. Vrin, 1999). See also *Pierre de Jean Olivi – Philosophe et théologien*, edited by Catherine König-Pralong, Olivier Ribordy, Tiziana Suarez-Nani, Scrinium Friburgense 29. (Berlin/New York: Walter de Gruyter, 2010). For orientation to Peter of John Olivi's Franciscan thought in particular, see David Flood, "The Theology of Peter John Olivi: A Search for a Theology and Anthropology of the Synoptic Gospels," in *The History of Franciscan Theology*, edited by Kenan B. Osborne (Saint Bonaventure, NY: The Franciscan Institute, 1994; reprinted 2007), 127-84.

In his lectures on Proverbs and Ecclesiastes Olivi generally follows his customary way of interpreting a biblical book by quoting other biblical passages and renowned authorities and providing the literal and mystical meaning of the text.[2] However, his lecture on Proverbs concludes with his comments on Proverbs 16. In other words, he offers no exegesis of Proverbs 17-31. Moreover, his comments on Proverbs 12-16 are largely limited to the citation of a biblical word or two plus "that is." For example, he comments on Proverbs 12:4a: "A *diligent woman*, that is, one who diligently does all the good things that are required of her."[3] This style of exegesis shows how Olivi could comment on many verses in a short compass, but it is not the summary style of exegesis that he employs in his *Lectura super Marcum*.

In his *Commentary on Isaiah* Olivi comments in his usual style on the first twelve chapters and then adopts a cursory style for Isaiah 13-66.[4] As far as I can determine, Olivi's cursory style on Isaiah 13-66 offers very little, if any, interpretive parallel for his *Lectura super Marcum*.

In his commentary on *The Song of Songs* Olivi follows his usual style of exposition by citing interpretive scripture passages and renowned authorities.[5] As an example I give Olivi's exposition of *The Song of Songs* 4:7: "*You are totally beautiful, my love, and there is no stain in you.* In this verse he commends her in a positive fashion as well as in a nega-

---

[2] *Petri Iohannis Olivi, Lectura super Proverbia et Lectura super Ecclesiasten*, edited by Johannes Schlageter, Collectio Oliviana 6 (Grottaferrata [Rome]: Collegium S. Bonaventurae, 2003).

[3] See *Lectura super Proverbia*, 289.

[4] *Peter of John Olivi on the Bible: Principia quinque in Sacram Scripturam, Postilla in Isaiam et in I ad Corinthios; Appendix: Quaestio de Oboedientia et Sermones duo de S. Francisco*, Franciscan Institute Publications Text Series 18, edited by David Flood and †Gedeon Gál. (St. Bonaventure, NY: The Franciscan Institute, 1997), 153-347. Olivi's comments on Isaiah 13-66 are found on 293-345. On p. 154 the editors observe: "Peter Olivi divides the whole book of Isaiah into three parts, the first one covering the first twelve chapters. Once he has finished with this first part, he stops his verse-by-verse analysis and goes over into a *lectura cursoria*."

[5] *Petri Iohannis Olivi, Expositio in Canticum Canticorum*, edited with a German translation by Johannes Schlageter, Collectio Oliviana 2 (Grottaferrata [Rome]: Collegium S. Bonaventurae, 1999).

tive manner. But since in this life no one is without sin according to what 1 John 1:8 says (*If we say that we do not have sin, we are deceiving ourselves*), how can he say that *there is no stain in you*? There is a threefold answer to this problem. The first is that he was speaking of mortal sin only. The second is the teaching of Augustine: by the very fact that those who continuously feel compunction for their venial sins, it is clear that their guilt and sin are washed away and are not in them. And this is how Pseudo-Gregory explains what Job 27:6 states: *for my heart does not reprove me during my entire life*.... The third answer also stems from Augustine who interprets Romans 8:24, *For we have been saved in hope*, to mean that by hope we have been washed clean from all stain. And this is what the Apostle says in Ephesians 5:27: *in order that he might present to himself the church in all her glory, not having stain or wrinkle*."[6]

In his *Commentary on Genesis* Peter of John Olivi follows his customary style of exposition by means of interpretive Scripture passages and citation of renowned authorities.[7] For example, in dealing with the words "in the beginning" of Genesis 1:1 he cites the authorities Hilary, Jerome, Augustine, and Pope Innocent III as well as the Letter to the Hebrews and Psalm 101.[8]

In his *Commentary on the Acts of the Apostles* Olivi also follows his customary style of exegesis by means of interpretive Scripture passages and citation of authorities.[9] For example, he interprets Acts 28:30 ("And for two full years he remained in his own hired lodging") by citing the Glossa, Ra-

---

[6] See *Expositio in Canticum Canticorum*, 200. I do not want to give the impression that in his exegesis of every verse Olivi offers such an array of Scripture passages and authorities. Ordinarily the citation of a biblical passage or of an authority is sufficient for Olivi's exegesis.

[7] See *Peter of John Olivi on Genesis*, edited by David Flood (St. Bonaventure, NY: Franciscan Institute Publications, 2007).

[8] See *Peter of John Olivi on Genesis*, 24-25.

[9] See *Peter of John Olivi on the Acts of the Apostles*, edited by David Flood, Franciscan Institute Publications Text Series 25. (St. Bonaventure, NY: Franciscan Institute Publications, 2001).

banus Maurus, Bede, as well as Romans 15:28 and 2 Timothy 4:16-17.[10]

Peter of John Olivi's *Commentary on 1 Corinthians* is unfinished and stops at 1 Corinthians 2.[11] Even in this very brief exposition it is evident that Olivi is following his customary modality of exegesis, as he quotes the Glossa five times and Anselm once and cites many interpretive Scripture passages.

In his *Lectura super Lucam* Olivi employs his customary way of exegesis.[12] I give as an example his exposition of Luke 2:7 ("and she laid him in a manger"). In his exegesis Olivi quotes Jerome twice and Isaiah 1:3 once.[13] In Olivi's very long and detailed commentary on Luke it is surprising to find an example of the summarizing exposition he uses in his *Commentary on Mark*. I translate the creative "headings" Olivi gives to these passages: "5:12-14. Third is perfect obedience not only to follow Christ, but also to subject oneself to the judgments of the priests and superiors. Thus he commanded the leper: 'Go, show yourself to the priest.... 6:1-5: Sixth is the freely available and delectable food of extreme poverty. This is shown in the rubbing of the ears of grain and in the eating of the grain.[14] 6:6-11: Seventh is the perfect strength to perform every good deed. This power is shown in

---

[10] See *Peter of John Olivi on the Acts of the Apostles*, 436-37.

[11] See *Peter of John Olivi on the Bible*, 350-64.

[12] See *Petri Iohannis Olivi Lectura super Lucam et Lectura super Marcum*, edited by Fortunato Iozzelli, Collectio Oliviana 5 (Grottaferrata [Rome]: Collegium S. Bonaventurae, 2010), 161-674.

[13] See *Petri Iohannis Olivi Lectura super Lucam et Lectura super Marcum*, 247-48. See also my annotated translation, "Peter of John Olivi on Luke 2:7," in *The Cord* 60 (2010): 401-05.

[14] Contrast the interpretation of Thomas Aquinas in *Catena Aurea: Commentary on the Four Gospels Collected from the Works of the Fathers*, Volume III St. Luke, translation edited by John Henry Cardinal Newman (London: The Saint Austin Press, 1999), 197: "Bede; For his disciples having no opportunity for eating because the multitudes thronged so, were naturally hungry, but by plucking the ears of corn they relieved their hunger, which is a mark of a strict habit of life, not seeking for prepared meats, but mere simple food."

the withered hand restored by Christ."[15] As we will see below, this style of giving an evocative "heading" to a passage is common coin in Olivi's *Commentary on Mark*.

Unfortunately, Peter of John Olivi's most famous biblical commentaries await publication. Warren Lewis awaits publication of his critical edition of the Latin of Olivi's *Commentary on the Apocalypse* and of an English translation of it.[16] A team of scholars is also concentrating great efforts in readying a critical edition of Olivi's *Commentary on Matthew's Gospel*.

OLIVI'S STYLE OF EXEGESIS

One of the first things readers note about Olivi's *Commentary on Mark* is how short it is. It is a mere nineteen pages in the critical edition.[17] In contrast Pseudo-Jerome's *Commentary on Mark* dedicates fifty-five columns to the Second Gospel.[18] Venerable Bede's *Commentary on Mark* spends a most generous 217 pages in its exposition.[19] Albert the Great, a contemporary of Olivi, devotes 422 pages to the Gospel of Mark.[20] In his opening paragraph Olivi even states: "... we propose to give a brief exposition of Mark, giving only a general and summary division of it, since he says few things that go beyond what is contained in Matthew ... we will touch in some measure on those things that he has added beyond

---

[15] See *Petri Iohannis Olivi Lectura super Lucam et Lectura super Marcum*, 331.

[16] The publication of the English translation by Franciscan Institute Publications will appear in a timely manner.

[17] See *Petri Iohannis Olivi Lectura super Lucam et Lectura super Marcum*, 691-709.

[18] See PL 30:589A-644A.

[19] See *Bedae Venerabilis Opera: Pars II Opera exegetica 3: Lucae Evangelivm Expositio, In Marci Evangelivm Expositio*, edited by D. Hurst, CCSL cxx (Turnhout: Brepols, 1960), 431-648.

[20] See *D. Alberti Magni Enarrationes in Matthaeum (XXI-XXVIII) – in Marcum*, Opera omnia XXI (Paris: Vives, 1894), 339-761.

what the others have."[21] But readers should not think that in Olivi's brevity of commentary there are few, if any, gems of interpretation. These gems will captivate and delight those who readjust their ways of interpreting Mark and follow Olivi's ways.

How does Olivi interpret Mark? One way is Olivi's often unique method of giving titles to what we today would call pericopes. Contemporary readers are used to finding such headings in their English translations. For example, The New Revised Standard Version has the following heading for Mark 7:24-30 "The Syrophoenician Woman's Faith."[22] By contrast Olivi in n. 10 gives this pericope the following long title: "Fifth is the avoidance of a person who is urging that it is a scandalous and failed approach to provide benefits to or associate with Gentiles and uneducated non-believers until their great faith in and devotion to God would demand another approach." Surely Olivi does not give any consideration to Mark 7:24-30 beyond this "title," but this title contains in a nutshell his interpretation of this passage. Shortness does not mean lack of depth. I give two more examples. The NRSV provides this title for Mark 9:38-41 "Another Exorcist."[23] In

---

[21] See *Petri Iohannis Olivi Lectura super Lucam et Lectura super Marcum*, 691. Olivi's principle on the interpretation of the Gospels is the fifth of his five principles on Sacred Scripture. See *Peter of John Olivi on the Bible*, 145: "Now the face of a human being fits Mark's Gospel, which primarily describes the preaching and truth of the abbreviated word, Christ. Thus, he commences with the preaching of John and with brevity of words, in a magisterial fashion, treats Christ's teaching and miracles." Here Olivi draws on the medieval teaching that the eternal Word became flesh and was thus abbreviated in a human life, in a particular place and culture. The abbreviated Word fits Mark's Gospel which does not contain many of Christ's teachings that are found in Matthew and Luke.

[22] See *The Holy Bible containing the Old and New Testaments, New Revised Standard Version: Catholic Edition* (Nashville: Catholic Bible Press, 1993), 42. See CCSL cxx, 434 for the chapter heading found in Bede's Commentary: "He delivers the Syrophoenician woman's daughter from a demon." See Albert the Great, *In Marcum*, 490: "He casts out a demon from the daughter of a Syrophoenician woman who persevered in her petitioning."

[23] See NRSV, 45. See CCSL cxx, 435 for the chapter heading found in Bede's Commentary: "He does not allow them to prohibit those who perform miracles in his name ..." See Albert the Great, *In Marcum*, 537:

contrast in n. 18 Olivi gives this title: "Second is the strong and diligent avoidance of giving scandal to anyone at all and over anything at all and of the gracious approbation and preservation of those things contributed by anyone at all, even though they are non-believers."[24] Would that Olivi had expounded on the meaning of this title, especially as it pertained to relationships with the Saracens! The NRSV titles Mark 14:3-9 as "The Anointing at Bethany."[25] For his part Olivi observes in n. 24: "The first point sets forth the traitorous procuring of Christ's capture and death and the motivating cause and reason for this wickedness which was the horrendous cupidity violently launched against Mary's wasting of precious ointment on Christ."[26] Indeed, in his brief "headings" Olivi is providing profound interpretation that does not follow the headings we use today.

Closely aligned to Olivi's method of giving succinct and often lapidary headings to pericopes is his method of dividing the text. Readers should remember that in the early Middle Ages the modern reference system of chapter and verse did not exist. In Olivi's case he divides the text by providing a broad division of it into three parts: Jesus' teaching, his passion and death, and his resurrection and ascension.[27] Then Olivi makes divisions within each part and subdivisions within those divisions. For example, in his treatment of Mark 4:35-6:6 Olivi writes in n. 8: "Now in the sixth principal section, which deals with the confirmation by miracles of the teaching already given, four miracles are detailed. The first

---

"Concerning the person who did not follow Jesus and was casting out a demon."

[24] Olivi's headings in n. 18 (Mark 9:30-10:52) are a parade example of this facet of his exegesis.

[25] See NRSV, 51. See CCSL cxx, 436 for the chapter heading found in Bede's Commentary: "About the alabaster jar of ointment or the betrayal of Judas the traitor..." See Albert the Great, *In Marcum*, 684: "Jesus is anointed by precious ointment by a woman while the disciples murmur about it."

[26] Does Olivi's Franciscan love of poverty and hatred of avarice blind him to the fact that "cupidity" is not mentioned in Mark?

[27] This method of dividing the text of Mark's Gospel into three major parts seems unique. It is not found in Jerome, Bede, or Hugh of St. Cher.

miracle ..." Through his division of the text Olivi separates the text of Mark's Gospel into pericopes upon which he then offers his often insightful headings.

Olivi employs another exegetical method when he introduces the imperative "note." See n. 20, 38, and 39. According to Fortunato Iozzelli, editor of the critical edition of Olivi's *Commentary on Mark*, this imperative is meant to arrest the reader's attention to a biblical passage and to provide a more or less deep interpretation of it.[28] Thus in n. 39 Olivi wants his readers to note that the expression "signs shall attend those who believe," etc. is open to a literal as well as a mystical interpretation.

In two instances Olivi employs the simple exegetical method of asking a question of the text. This is not the scholastic *quaestio*, but is yet another means of arresting the reader's attention. In n. 11 Olivi asks: "but why 'did he put his fingers into the ears' of the deaf man and 'touch his tongue' with his spittle?" In the remainder of n. 11 Olivi answers his question. At the beginning of n. 12 Olivi asks: "Now why 'did he sigh' while performing this cure?" In three sentences Olivi gives his answer.[29]

If readers come to Olivi's *Commentary on Mark* for spiritual nourishment, they will not be disappointed. For example, Olivi's expositions of Mark 4:26-29 and 8:22-26, passages unique to Mark, are largely mystical. See also his extensive spiritual interpretations of Mark 9:30-10:52.

But Olivi's goals for his commentary go beyond providing spiritual nourishment. He wants to give his resolution of some of the difficulties the text of Mark presented.[30] In deal-

---

[28] See *Petri Iohannis Olivi Lectura super Lucam et Lectura super Marcum*, 681. See also Gilbert Dahan, *l'exégèse chrétienne de la Bible en Occident medieval XIIe-XIVe siècle* (Paris: Cerf, 1999), 129-31.

[29] See Dahan, 131-34. On 122-41 Dahan presents what he considers the simple forms or the microstructures of exegesis. These include the Glossae, the imperatival "note," the question, the distinction, the concatenation of verses, and the amassing of exegetical authorities. In his Commentary on Mark's Gospel Olivi is very much at home with a number of these microstructures.

[30] In doing so, Olivi may have anticipated some aspects of the modern historical critical method. For the use of that methodology in interpreting

ing with Mark 1:1-13, Olivi has to resolve the question of why Mark said he is quoting Isaiah when he was really quoting both Isaiah and Malachi (n. 3). In n. 10 Olivi is constrained to figure out Mark's geography in 7:31: "He came to the Sea of Galilee through the midst of the district of the Decapolis." In n. 18 Olivi has to reconcile differences between Mark 10:1-12 and Matthew 19:1-12, esp. what Matthew said in verses 10-12 about the expediency of not marrying. Olivi devotes his longest paragraph by far in n. 20 to the question of the exact day on which Christ expelled the sellers from the Temple.[31] In n. 25 Olivi resolves the question of when the first day of Unleavened Bread occurred. In n. 29 he has to resolve the question of the meaning of Christ's words: "Sleep now and take your rest. It is enough." Finally, in n. 38 he delves into the meaning of Mark 16:14 "Finally, he appeared" and asks: Is this the last appearance on the first day of resurrection or the very last one Christ made to his disciples while they were at table?

As far as I can determine, there is very little, if any, of Olivi's apocalyptic theology of history in his *Commentary on Mark*.[32] For example, in his interpretation of the parables in Mark 4 Olivi has none of the interpretation he gave to the seven parables in Matthew 13. I quote from Kevin Madigan's translation of Olivi: "'Note that all of the parables [i.e., each individually] describe the course of faith and of the church or New Testament. In addition, [as a group] the first two have to do with the beginning of the sowing of faith and of the church. The next two, namely, the Mustard Seed and the Leaven, have to do with its expansion. The last three have to do with its end. The first two of these deal with the renovation of evangelical poverty and perfection and the last with

---

Mark's Gospel, see Adela Yarbro Collins, *Mark: A Commentary*, Hermeneia (Minneapolis: Fortress, 2007).

[31] Olivi also uses the imperative "note" here.

[32] See n. 22 below where twice Olivi reads "anti-Christs" whereas the Vulgate has *pseudochristi* ("false christs"). However, there is no other indication of Olivi's apocalyptic theology of history in his interpretation of Mark 13 in n. 22.

the final conversion of the world."'[33] Readers can well pose the question: Granted that Olivi wrote his commentary on Mark after he authored his commentary on Matthew, why does he not interpret Mark 4 and Mark 13 apocalyptically as he did with their Matthean parallels? Answers to this question will be speculative, but one suggests itself. Even though Olivi authored his commentary on Mark after his apocalyptic commentary on Matthew, it gives an indication of his earlier non-apocalyptic interpretation.

Finally, one cannot read Olivi's *Commentary on Mark* without being struck by his use of numbers, e.g., the first part of Mark's Gospel has twelve sections; the tenth principal section has seven counsels. Is Olivi's use of such numbers a mnemonic device? Or is he enhancing his interpretation of the Gospel by means of these perfect numbers? It seems to me that the answer to these two questions is not either/or, but both/and.[34]

MIRACLES

Since Christ's miracles feature so prominently in Mark's Gospel, Peter of John Olivi cannot avoid them and has to interpret them. Most often he gives them a brief interpreta-

---

[33] See Kevin Madigan, *Olivi and the Interpretation of Matthew in the High Middle Ages* (Notre Dame, IN: University of Notre Dame Press, 2003), 85.

[34] A helpful basic book on the meaning of numbers in the Middle Ages is Vincent Foster Hopper, *Medieval Number Symbolism: Its Sources, Meaning, and Influence on Thought and Expression* (Mineola, NY: Dover, 2000 [1938]). See further Gilbert Dahan, "Arithmologie et exégèse: Un chapitre du *De scripturis* de Hugues de Saint-Victor," *Prisma* 8 (1992): 155-73, reprinted in Gilbert Dahan, *Lire la Bible au Moyen Âge: Essais d'herméneutique médiévale* (Genève: Droz, 2009), 135-60. Henri de Lubac, *Exégèse médiéval: Les quâtre sens de l'écriture*. Seconde Partie II (Paris: Aubier, 1964): 7-40. See Madigan, *Olivi*, 83-84 for Olivi's use of numbers in his *Commentary on Matthew*. On p. 83 Madigan writes: "Throughout the commentary, Olivi finds in those texts which arrange themselves in groups of seven a prophecy of all of church history, including the renewal of evangelical poverty in the sixth period." Such a usage is absent in Olivi's *Commentary on Mark*.

tion. More extensive, and mystical/allegorical, treatment is reserved for the two miracles that are unique to Mark. I first list the miracles that Olivi considers, giving to the extent possible, some of his incisive one-line interpretations. Next I consider Olivi's treatment of Mark's two unique miracles: 7:31-37 and 8:22-26. Finally, I look at how Olivi interprets Mark's emphasis on Christ as a miracle worker and how he views the disciples and the faithful, who in general and in Olivi's time, continue Christ's miracles.

LISTING OF MIRACLES

In n. 1 Olivi considers Mark 1:23-28 (cure of a demoniac) and Mark 1:29-31 (cure of Simon's mother-in-law).[35]

In n. 8 he considers four miracles: Mark 4:35-40 (Christ's calming of the storm on the lake); Mark 5:1-20 (cure of the Gerasene demoniac); Mark 5:21-43 (cure of the woman with a hemorrhage and the resuscitation of a twelve year old girl).

In n. 9 he portrays Christ's sending of the apostles to whom he gave power over unclean spirits (Mark 6:7).

In n. 10 he narrates how Christ abundantly fed the 5,000 (Mark 6:34-44), calmed the stormy sea (Mark 6:44-52),[36] and cured many (Mark 6:53-56).

In nn. 10-12 he interprets at length, especially in a mystical reading, a miracle that is unique to Mark, namely, the curing of the deaf-mute (Mark 7:31-37).[37]

In n. 13 he treats Christ's superabundant feeding of the 4,000 (Mark 8:1-9) and the Pharisees' demand for a sign (8:11-12).

In nn. 13-14 he presents an elaborate mystical interpretation of another miracle that is unique to this Gospel,

---

[35] For some reason Olivi skips the miracles of Mark 1:40-45 (cure of a leper) and Mark 2:1-12 (cure of a paralytic).

[36] For some reason Olivi does not mention that this miracle also highlights Christ's walking on water.

[37] In n. 10 Olivi seems to downplay Christ's actual healing of the daughter of the Syrophoenician woman (Mark 7:24-30) and deals with the mission to non-believers.

namely, Christ's healing of the blind man at Bethsaida (Mark 8:22-26).

In n. 17 he treats Christ's healing of a possessed boy (Mark 9:13-28) and his instruction to his disciples that they can obtain such power by prayer and fasting.

At the end of n. 18 Olivi stresses that Christ's miracle for a certain blind man showed the power and approbation of the man's faithful and persistent prayer (Mark 10:46-52).

In n. 19 Olivi interprets Christ's cursing of and the withering up of the fig tree (Mark 11:12-14, 20-22) in two ways. The withered fig tree is a type of Jewish sterility and wickedness. The power to work miracles stems from solid faith and faithful and devout prayer.[38]

In n. 32 Olivi accentuates the miracles of Mark 15:20-39. Olivi interprets the inscription, The King of the Jews (Mark 15:26), to point to Christ's "triumphal death." Christ's expiration by means of the miracle of his loud voice leads to the centurion's proclamation that he was truly the Son of God. This miracle is augmented by the complete rending of the Temple curtain before the Holy of Holies (Mark 15:37-39).

In n. 39 Olivi gives a literal and a mystical interpretation of the words, "the signs that shall attend those who believe" (Mark 16:17).

TWO MIRACLES UNIQUE TO MARK

As we take a brief look at Olivi's interpretation of these two miracles, we will notice that he treats the literal meaning quickly and spends the lion's share of his time on the mystical meaning. Olivi devotes most of nn. 10-12 to his interpretation of Christ's cure of the deaf-mute (Mark 7:31-37) and uses the technique of asking questions: why "did he put his fingers into the ears" of the deaf man and "touch his

---

[38] In n. 22 Olivi does not mention "the signs and wonders" performed by false christs and false prophets (Mark 13:22).

tongue"? After giving the literal explanation that these actions showed in a more evident manner Christ's power, Olivi gives a number of mystical interpretations. For example, through the spittle "is signified the power of taste and the power to interpret the marvels of our God and of our faith, among which is the complete and integral confession of sins, by which the justice and mercy of God are commended" (n. 11). Olivi answers the question of why Christ sighed (v.34) on the basis of Christ's natures as God and human. Through his teaching and example of taking the deaf-mute aside Christ shows that one must avoid human glory (n. 10).

In nn. 13-14 Olivi interprets Christ's two-stage cure of the blind man of Bethsaida (Mark 8:22-26). Why does Christ lead the blind man outside the village? He wants to give "exemplary teaching about how to avoid vain glory when performing miracles of this kind" (n. 13). Why did Christ not cure the blind man completely at once as he cured others? There is a dual reason. "The first reason is literal, so that he might show that there is not just one way of curing.... The second reason is mystical..." (n. 14). I quote the third mystical meaning Olivi provides. It is from the Glossa:

A person who has been leading a life of foolishness does not immediately know how to discern between good and evil, faith and perfidy, sincerity and simulation. Light is given to that person by the second laying on of hands so that the person may discern matters of this kind and even discern all that is to be believed in and hoped for and fled from.

CHRIST AND HIS FOLLOWERS AS MIRACLE WORKERS IN MARK'S GOSPEL

For Olivi Christ's miracles confirm his teaching (see, e.g., n. 2). They also lead to belief in him. Christ's public ministry begins with miracles, and his life ends with a miracle. What Olivi says about the loud cry with which Christ dies is a quasi-summary of Olivi's teaching on miracles: "Ninth is Christ's expiration by means of the miracle of a loud voice and the centurion's proclamation, made because of this miracle, that he was truly the Son of God" (n. 32).

But Christ is not the only one to perform miracles in Mark's Gospel. Christ gives his apostles power over unclean spirits (6:7). The disciples may obtain power over demons through prayer and fasting (9:28). In his interpretation of Jesus' miracle of the withering of the fig tree (Mark 11:12-14, 20-26), Olivi comments: "... the obtaining and performing of miracles of whatever type and even the obtaining of all gifts are promised to those who have solid faith and engage in faithful and devout prayer ..." (n. 19). In n. 37 Olivi mentions Christ's "gift to the faithful of the power to work miracles." The literal meaning of Mark 16:17 ("signs shall attend those who believe") is that it refers to "those who perfectly believe and ... to signs that are necessary or very expedient in confirming the faith" (n. 39). In brief, the preaching of Christ's disciples is confirmed by their miracles (nn. 34, 39). From these interpretations and the exemplary teaching "about how to avoid vain glory when performing miracles of this kind" (n. 13; see n. 10), I would venture to ask whether Olivi was addressing some situations in his own day when perfect believers were performing miracles to confirm their teaching. Such miracles should not lead to vanity and glorying in public acclaim.

PRESENTATION OF CHRIST

Olivi's presentation of Christ is linked to Christ as a miracle worker. Christ shows his "provident and powerful divine guidance" when he supplies abundant food for the 5,000 (n. 2). Christ "sighs" in his human nature over the miserable condition of humans (n. 12) and then proceeds to cure the deaf-mute through his divine nature. Christ's life ends with the miracle of his loud cry (n. 32). The centurion is won to faith in Jesus as the Son of God by this miracle of his loud cry at death (n. 32).

But Christ is more than a miracle worker in Mark's Gospel. He is the judge at the final judgment. Olivi comments: "Fifth is the proof given by the Psalmist for Christ's power to judge as co-ruler with God the Father" (n. 21). He has majesty (n. 15) and glory (n. 17). Further, Christ's future passion is "the exemplar and causative perfection of all the counsels" (n. 18).

In three major sections Mark's Gospel presents Jesus as a teacher: Mark 4:1-34; Mark 9:29-10:45; Mark 11:15-13:37. In these sections there are no miracles. In n. 1 Olivi states he will touch in some measure on those things that Mark has added beyond what Matthew has. Accordingly, Olivi devotes considerable space in nn. 5-6 to Mark's unique parable of the seed growing by itself (Mark 4:26-29). In n. 5 Olivi sets forth allegorical, moral, and anagogical interpretations of this parable. For example, "now that the seed grows ... signifies allegorically the power of divine grace, that grows under the surface and advances in multiple ways in subjects without the continued cooperation of teachers" (n. 5). In n. 6 Olivi interprets the "blade," "ear," and full grain to mean the gradual threefold perfection through grace.

Even though Christ's teachings in Mark 9:30-10:45 are not unique to Mark, Olivi's interpretations are unique in their persuasive power. Almost each interpretation bears full quotation. Here are two of Olivi's interpretations. He comments on Mark 9:29-31 in n. 18: Christ's "future passion is introduced as the exemplar and causative perfection of all the counsels." In n. 18 he interprets 9:37-49 in this manner: "Second is the strong and diligent avoidance of giving scandal to anyone at all and over anything at all and of the gracious approbation and preservation of those things contributed by anyone at all, even though they are non-believers."

A most arresting feature of Olivi's interpretation of Mark 11:15-13:37 is his stress on Christ as judge. For example, in n. 21 Olivi interprets Mark 12:35-37 in this vein: "Fifth is the proof given by the Psalmist for Christ's power to judge as co-ruler with God the Father ..."

THE PHARISEES, SCRIBES, AND JEWS

In Mark's Gospel the people who largely resist faith in Christ and his miracles and reject his teachings are the Pharisees, Scribes, and the Jews. In this regard Olivi was heir to the anti-Judaism of his time.[39] I refer readers to nn. 4, 10, 13, 18, 19, 21, 24, and 31 for Olivi's most salient comments against Jewish non-believers in Christ. I give three examples. In n. 10 Olivi comments on Mark 7:1-23: "Fourth is the nullifying or abolishing of superstitious cleanliness and consequently the explication and approbation of what truly and necessarily has to be observed ..." In n. 19 Olivi interprets Christ's miracle of the withering of the fig tree in this light: "Fourth is the cursing and withering up of the fig tree as a type of Jewish sterility and wickedness ..." Finally, in n. 21 Olivi explicates Christ's parable of the vineyard thus: "First is the just ruin of the Jews as the perverse workers of the vineyard of the Lord and the introduction of other workers to care for the vineyard." What Olivi says about the Jews in his Commentary on Mark's Gospel is not his final word. He presents a more positive view in his *Commentary on the Apocalypse*.[40]

---

[39] For a more detailed consideration of the theological, ecclesiastical, cultural, and political contexts of Olivi's anti-Judaism, see *St. Bonaventure's Commentary on the Gospel of Luke Chapters 9-16*, with an introduction, translation and notes by Robert J. Karris, WSB VIII/2 (Saint Bonaventure, NY: Franciscan Institute Publications, 2003), xiii-xxxiii.

[40] See Warren Lewis, "Freude, Freude? Die Wiederentdeckung der Freude im 13 Jahrhundert: Olivis 'Lectura super Apocalipsim' als Blick auf die Endzeit" in *Ende und Vollendung: Eschatologische Perspektiven im Mittelalter*, ed. Jan A. Aertsen and Martin Pickavé, Miscellanea Mediaevalia 29 (Berlin/New York: Walter de Gruyter, 2002), 657-83, esp. 675-76. See, too, how Robert E. Lerner evaluates the view of Olivi and others about the Jews in his *The Feast of Saint Abraham: Medieval Millenarians and the Jews* (Philadelphia: University of Pennsylvania Press, 2001), 120: "to avoid clumsiness I have occasionally fallen back on the term philo-Judaism, but the more accurate phraseology for the stance of my subjects would be 'relatively more benign attitude towards the Jews than the late medieval

THE DISCIPLES AND DISCIPLES WHO ARE FRANCISCANS

In many of Olivi's comments about Christ's disciples he seems to have left behind the historical disciples of the first century and is talking to his present day disciples. Further, it seems that many of the present day disciples he is addressing are Franciscans who profess the evangelical counsels and are listening to him lecture on Mark's Gospel in a Franciscan *studium*. I give some examples. In n. 4 Olivi comments on Mark 3:31-35: "Ninth is the rejection of carnal concern for one's parents and the embracing of totally spiritual matters for spiritual people ..." In n. 6 Olivi comments on blade, ear, and full grain of Mark 4:28 by means of the three stages of spiritual life. In n. 9 Olivi explains Christ's missionary command to his apostles "to take nothing for their journey," etc. (Mark 6:8-9) as "the declaration of evangelical poverty." In nn. 10, 14 Olivi is concerned that present day disciples who might perform miracles should not fall prey to vainglory. The heart of Olivi's teaching about the spiritual or evangelical life occurs in n. 18 where he comments on Mark 9:30-10:45. Christ's instructions to his disciples concern the perfection of his counsels. "The perfection of Christ's counsels is to be assumed as soon as possible after one has attained the first use of reason or after one has been converted to the faith." Olivi interprets acceptance of Christ's invitation to the rich man (Mark 10:17-31) as "assent to highest and universal poverty." To counter the disciples who want first places in his kingdom Christ gives them his example of serving and giving his life as a ransom for many (Mark 10:35-45). Olivi remarks: "... he again adds the counsel of evangelical humiliation, even until death ..." Is Olivi's depiction of Christ's "triumphal death" (n. 32) another indication of his Franciscan soul? Finally, in n. 35 Olivi underscores the role of the disciple Mary of Magdala who receives the risen "Christ's primordial appearance."

Christian norm.'" See further Robert Lerner, "Peter Olivi on the Conversion of the Jews," in *Pierre de Jean Olivi (1248-1298)*, 207-16.

SOURCES

At first blush it seems that Olivi doesn't use many sources. He refers to the Glossa ordinaria in nn. 10 and 14 (3x). In n. 20 he refers to Peter Comestor. In nn. 29 and 38 he cites Augustine. In n. 39 he refers to Gregory the Great.[41] Yet upon further probing I have discovered that Olivi often follows the commentary of Venerable Bede. In doing this, he was following good company, for the Glossa ordinaria on Mark often cited Bede. In the footnotes I have set forth the instances I have been able to detect where Olivi follows Bede, but does not indicate that he is doing so. In only one instance might Olivi make use of the *Commentary on Mark* by Hugh of St. Cher, and that is in his comments on Mark 1:2-3.[42]

One might look at Olivi's use of sources from yet another angle: What sources does he rarely or never use? The Commentary on Mark's Gospel by Hugh of St. Cher runs to seventy folio pages and was very popular, but Olivi may quote just once from this Dominican Cardinal's exposition.[43] As far as I can ascertain, he does not consult the *Commentary on Mark* that in his day was attributed to Jerome.[44] As far as I can determine, there was no cross fertilization with the *Commen-*

---

[41] Gregory devotes only two of his forty homilies to Mark's Gospel. He comments on Mark 16:1-7 in Homily 21 and on Mark 16:14-20 in Homily 29.

[42] In his relationship to Hugh of St. Cher's *Commentary on Mark*, Olivi distances himself from his teacher, Bonaventure of Bagnoregio, who is heavily indebted to Hugh of St. Cher in his Commentary on Luke's Gospel. For a snapshot of the numerous occasions when Bonaventure is indebted to Hugh of St. Cher, see the cumulative indices under "Hugh of St. Cher" in *St. Bonaventure's Commentary on the Gospel of Luke Chapters 17-24*, with an introduction, translation and notes by Robert J. Karris, WSB VIII/3 (St. Bonaventure, NY: Franciscan Institute Publications, 2004), 2446-49. See *Hugonis de Sancto Charo ... Tomus Sextus in Evangelia secundum Matthaeum, Lucam, Marcum & Joannem* (Venice: Nicolas Pezzana, 1732), 90-125v.

[43] See *Hugonis de Sancto Charo*, 91 on Mark 1:2-3.

[44] See *Expositio in Evangelium secundum Marcum* in PL 30:560D-644A. See now *Expositio evangelii secundum Marcum*, ed. Michael Cahill, CCSL 82 (Turnhout: Brepols, 1997). See also *The First Commentary on Mark: An Annotated Translation*, translated and edited by Michael Cahill (New York: Oxford University Press, 1998).

tary on Mark written by Albert the Great (d. 1280).[45] After delving into the relationship between Olivi's *Commentary on Mark* and Thomas Aquinas's *Commentary on Mark*, I have detected no dependence of Olivi on Aquinas.[46]

DATE OF OLIVI'S COMMENTARY ON MARK'S GOSPEL

After a discussion of the dating of Olivi's commentaries on the Gospels, Fortunato Iozzelli concludes: "In the final analysis, in his commentaries on the four gospels, Olivi has followed this order: Matthew and John (1279-1282), then Mark and Luke (some years before 1295)."[47]

A Word about the Appendix

In an Appendix I provide translations of Albert the Great's commentary on passages that are unique to Mark. It is my hope that these commentaries will help readers to contrast

---

[45] See Albert the Great, *In Marcum*, 341-761. I will occasionally place Albert the Great's interpretation of a Markan passage in a footnote so that readers may compare and contrast it with Olivi's exposition.

[46] See *S. Thomae Aquinatis Catena Aurea in Quatuor Evangelia*, Volume I (Turin: Marietti, 1938), 467-617. See also *Catena Aurea,* Volume II. Occasionally I will place Thomas Aquinas's interpretation of a Markan passage in a footnote for the sake of comparison and contrast. Olivi's non-use of Aquinas's *Catena Aurea* in commenting on Mark's Gospel stands in contrast with his frequent use of the same in his *Commentary on Matthew*. For Olivi's use of *Catena Aurea* in general see Louis-J. Bataillon, "Olivi utilisateur de la *Catena aurea* de Thomas d'Aquin" in *Pierre de Jean Olivi (1248-1298)*, 115-20. With particular reference to Olivi's use of Aquinas in commenting on Matthew's Gospel see Madigan, *Olivi*, 2: "... Olivi borrows ideas from no other contemporary exegetical writing in his Matthew commentary as liberally as he does from that innocuous work (*Catena Aurea*), a papally commissioned mosaic of unthreatening opinions collated from the writings of the orthodox fathers."

[47] See *Lectura super Lucam et Lectura super Marcum*, 678. Madigan, *Olivi*, 73 gives the same general dating for Olivi's *Commentary on Mark*: "... we are able to say with some confidence that the Matthew commentary was written either in the academic years 1279-80 or 1280-81, probably the former. At the very least, then, it is clear that the John commentary was written sometime after 1280 and the Mark-Luke commentary sometime after that."

and compare the expositions of the two contemporaries: Albert the Great and Peter of John Olivi.

A WORD ABOUT THIS TRANSLATION

My goals in translation have been readability and fidelity. I accentuate the literal rather than the literary. At times when Olivi's text is unclear, I move into a dynamic equivalency style of translation in an attempt to convey his meaning. For greater readability I have introduced paragraph numbers into Olivi's text and have denoted sub-points, however tiny, as "sub-sections." In the extensive Table of Contents interested readers will find a detailed roadmap to Olivi's Commentary, replete with indications of "principal sections," "sub-sections," and four excursus. In the indices readers will find a ready reference to key biblical passages and authorities.

A Word of Thanks

I want to thank Professors David Flood, Warren Lewis, and Joshua Benson for reading my annotated translation and improving it by their suggestions and corrections. Of course, I alone am responsible for the infelicities that remain.

The Franciscan Institute thanks the generous donors who have helped this volume see the light of day.

Dedication

This volume is dedicated to Fr. Michael F. Cusato, O.F.M.
for his many insightful writings
and his creative initiatives
to keep the Franciscan vision alive and well
in the twenty-first century.

PETER OF JOHN OLIVI
ON THE GOSPEL OF MARK[1]

PART I: THE COURSE OF CHRIST'S PREACHING[2]

1) In our previous commentaries on the Gospels of Matthew and John, we have virtually touched on everything in the Gospels of Mark and Luke. From these same commentaries it is sufficiently plain and evident how to exegete what remains. So in this commentary we propose to give a brief explanation of Mark and to provide only a general and summary division of it, since he says few things that go beyond what is contained in Matthew. As we did in our commentary on Luke, we will touch in some measure on those things that Mark has added beyond what the others have.[3]

2) Mark begins with Christ's preaching and treats it in twelve principal sections. First, he deals with the mission of his predecessor.[4] Second he narrates Christ's baptism where the text reads: "And it came to pass in those days."[5] Third is Christ's temptation where the text says: "And immediately

---

[1] See *Peter Iohannis Olivi, Lectura super Lucam et Lectura super Marcum*, 691-709.

[2] Mark 1:1-13:37.

[3] See Olivi's extensive treatment of the following passages unique to Mark: Mark 4:26-29 in n. 5-6; Mark 7:31-37 in n. 10-12; Mark 8:22-26 in n. 13-14 below. Apparently Olivi does not deem it necessary or appropriate to comment on small features that are uniquely Markan. For example, he does not exegete Mark 14:51-52 which tells of a young man who flees naked from Gethsemane.

[4] See Mark 1:2-9, 14.

[5] See Mark 1:9.

the Spirit drove him into the desert."[6] Fourth are the call and the election of the disciples where the text states: "Now after John was handed over."[7] At this point Mark begins to give considerable and special attention to Christ's preaching. Fifth is Christ's teaching to the crowds in parables where chapter 4 says: "And again Jesus began to teach."[8] Sixth is the confirmation of the aforesaid teaching by miracles where it is said in the same chapter: "And he said to them on that day when evening had come."[9] Seventh deals with the mission of the disciples to preach or of the command that they exercise their apostolic office where chapter 6 states: "And he called the Twelve."[10] The eighth focuses on Christ's provident and powerful divine guidance where the same chapter says: "And when he landed Jesus saw a large crowd."[11] The ninth presents the manifestation of the future and magnificent glory of Christ where chapter 9 says: "And after six days Jesus took, etc."[12] The tenth considers the perfection of the evangelical counsels where the same chapter states: "Now he was teaching his disciples and was saying to them: The Son of Man will be handed over."[13] The eleventh treats the royal honor shown him publicly and with great solemnity where chapter 11 states: "And when Jesus drew near to Jerusalem."[14] The twelfth concerns the final and judicial recompense of the good and the evil where chapter 12 says: "And Jesus began to speak to them in parables: A man planted a vineyard, etc."[15]

---

[6] See Mark 1:12.

[7] See Mark 1:14.

[8] See Mark 4:1.

[9] See Mark 4:35.

[10] See Mark 6:7.

[11] See Mark 6:34 which continues: "... and had compassion on them, because they were like sheep without a shepherd. And he began to teach them many things."

[12] See Mark 9:1.

[13] See Mark 9:30.

[14] See Mark 11:1. I translate the Vulgate: "And when they drew near to Jerusalem."

[15] See Mark 12:1.

3) Mark 1:1-13. The details of the first three principal sections are brief and relatively clear. He states what "the beginning of the Gospel," that is, of the preaching, "of Jesus Christ" is. It began with the preaching of John "as it is written in Isaiah the prophet: the voice of one crying," etc. But he inserted these words from Malachi the prophet: "Behold, I am sending my messenger," etc. as if they were written in Isaiah.[16] These words have to be understood as the insertion of a brief discourse. The evangelist's purpose is to give testimony to John's preaching by means of the authority of Isaiah. It is the same reason why John himself used this text. Since in this matter Malachi agrees with and expresses himself a little clearer by using the term "messenger" or that a messenger is to be sent to go "before" Christ, the evangelist inserted the word of Malachi between stating Isaiah's name and giving his actual testimony. But over and above this explanation it could be said that the evangelist takes all the prophets in the same way because of the one prophetic spirit which was in them.[17] Alternatively, it could be said that Isaiah spoke the very word of Malachi in as far as their statements said the same thing.[18]

---

[16] See Isa 40:3 and Mal 3:1.

[17] See *Bedae Venerabilis Opera: Pars II Opera exegetica 3: In Lvcae Evangelivm Expositio, In Marci Evangelivm Expositio*, edited by D. Hurst, CCSL cxx (Turnhout: Brepols, 1960), 439, where Bede quotes Augustine, but changes Augustine's text which deals with Matthew referring to Jeremiah when the prophet should be Zachariah in Matt 27:9-10 and compares this change to Mark changing Malachi to Isaiah: "For it may have been the case that when Mark was composing his Gospel, the word Isaiah occurred to his mind, in accordance with a familiar experience, instead of Malachi.... That some idea was thus conveyed of the marvelous manner in which all the holy prophets, speaking in one spirit, continued in perfect unison with each other in their utterances ... and of looking upon their individual communications as also those of the whole body, and on their collective communications as also those of each separately." See Book III, ch.7, n.30 in *Sancti Avreli Avgvstini De consensv Evangelistarvm*, edited by Franciscvs Weihrich, CSEL xliii (Vienna: F. Tempsky/Leipzig: G. Freytag, 1894), 305-06. See also NPNF, Series 1, Volume 6, 181-92.

[18] See the commentary of Bede on Mark 1:3 in CCSL cxx, 439: "... rather it is to be understood that although these words from Malachi are not found in Isaiah, their sense is found in Isaiah and in many other places and is most manifest in what is added here: *A voice crying in the wilder-*

4) Mark 1:14-3:35. Now relative to the fourth principal section, which is the call of the disciples, the evangelist first sets forth the call of the four primary disciples who are called on the same day and in pairs.[19] Second he sets forth the spread of Christ's reputation to many by means of his wonderful teaching and powerful miracles where the text states: "And they entered Capernaum."[20] In Capernaum special mention is made of two miracles. The first was more public to attract all the people whereas the second was more private and meant to give special strengthening to the four disciples just called.[21] Third he states that many were coming to Christ and were devoted to him because of his teachings and miracles where text states: "Now when it was evening."[22] He also describes the wicked zeal that certain scribes have in opposing Christ. Fourth he sets forth the calling of Matthew the publican where chapter 2 states: "And as he was passing along, he saw Levi of Alphaeus," that is, the son of Alphaeus.[23] Fifth he presents the condescending compassion of Christ towards the publicans, his disciples, and the sick and contrasts it with the uncompassionate complaining of the Pharisees whom he silences where the text reads: "And the scribes and the Pharisees, seeing that he ate with publicans," etc.[24] Sixth he sets forth the Pharisees' most virulent attack against Christ and

---

ness: *Prepare the way of the Lord. Make straight his paths.* Who would not see how great a concordance there is between both statements?" Is Olivi also indebted to Hugh of St. Cher? See Hugh of St. Cher, 91: "Porphyry the heretic howls that the Gospels do not speak the truth because Mark says that the authority behind this statement is Isaiah when it is really Malachi. Now the solution is twofold, for Isaiah says the same thing, but in different words.... Second all the prophets said the same thing, but one said it explicitly while another said it implicitly." See Collins, *Mark*, 136 who gives three contemporary possible solutions to this problem, e.g., "another possibility is that he (Mark) created the composite citation himself and attributed the whole to Isaiah, since he was better known than Malachi."

[19] See Mark 1:16-20.

[20] See Mark 1:21.

[21] See Mark 1:23-28 and Mark 1:29-31.

[22] See Mark 1:32. Olivi skips the miracles of 1:40-45 (a leper) and of 2:1-12 (a paralytic).

[23] See Mark 2:13-17.

[24] See Mark 2:16.

their caution in withdrawing from him. He also contrasts their wickedness with the growing testimony given him by the crowds and even the demons. This is contained in Mark 3 below: "And the Pharisees went out."[25] Seventh he presents the election of the twelve disciples to apostleship where the text states: "And going up a mountain."[26] Eighth he sets forth the horrible scorn that both Christ's own and the Pharisees give to Christ where the text says: "And they came to the house."[27] Ninth he presents the rejection of carnal concern for one's parents and the embracing of totally spiritual matters for spiritual people where the text reads: "And his mother and brethren came to him."[28]

5) Mark 4:1-34. In the fifth principal section, which deals with teaching or instruction through parables, five detailed parables are recounted. The first parable concerns the seed and the varied ways it can die or grow. The second parable deals with the putting of the lamp on the lamp stand to give clear illumination. The third parable focuses on measuring generously to others or the proportional recompense involved for those who measure well or poorly.

6) The fourth parable is one found only in Mark and deals with the spontaneous, unnoticed, and gradual growth of seeds sown on the ground and finally their harvest.[29] That the seed grows without the farmer's knowledge or while he is sleeping or engaged in or planning other activities signifies allegorically the power of divine grace. Grace grows under the surface and matures in multiple ways in subjects with-

---

[25] See Mark 3:6 which continues: "... and immediately took counsel with the Herodians against him, how they might do away with him."

[26] See Mark 3:13.

[27] See Mark 3:20.

[28] See Mark 3:31-35. See Albert the Great, *In Marcum*, 416: "Here (Mark 3:31-35) is the final part of this dispute. This part shows that one must not retreat from divine work for the sake of carnal affection.... [third] is Christ's determination that he would not withdraw from spiritual matters for the sake of carnal matters."

[29] The expansive treatment that Olivi gives to this unique Markan parable seems equivalent to an excursus.

out the continued assistance of teachers. The moral meaning is that the seed grows abundantly by itself, without anyone paying attention to it, just as one's own body grows without one's noticing it. Of course, a person provides food for himself by feeding his body. Yet such care does not make his body grow. Anagogically this means that God, who is the principal sower, so secretly provides for our growth that it seems that God is asleep or taking care of other matters. "Blade" and "ear" and fruit or full grain[30] in the "ear" refer to the three stages of gradual perfection brought about by grace.[31] The first is the blooming and tender exercise of the virtues, which usually occurs in novices. Second are the sending out and the lifting up of fragile and fitting desires to bring about the full grain of perfection. Third is the perfect formation in perfection itself.[32] God, in leading us through death out of this life,

---

[30] See Mark 4:28.

[31] See Stephen L. Wailes, *Medieval Allegories of Jesus' Parables*, UCLA Center for Medieval and Renaissance Studies 23 (Berkeley: University of California Press, 1987), 200-02 where he treats in his n. 24 what he calls "The Patient Husbandman." Wailes notes on 200-01 that the dominant interpretation was that of the Gloss which says that "the three stages of development – blade, ear, and grain – represent fear, penitence, and charity..." See Albert the Great, *In Marcum*, 433: "It comes to fruition in stages. First is the blade, a vigorous faith ... the Glossa calls the blade fear.... After a robust faith it produces shoots of virtues or after fear it produces penitence.... Therefore, it produces the ear after a robust faith or fear. The full grain comes in meritorious work that is done by charity." On 201 Wailes states: "For Gregory the blade, ear, and grain simply represent the beginning, furtherance, and completion of this moral process." See Homily II, 3.5 in *Sancti Gregorii Magni Homiliae in Hiezechihelem Prophetam*, edited by Marcus Adriaen, CCSL cxlii (Turnhout: Brepols, 1971), 240: "To produce the blade is the beginning of doing good; this stage is characterized by tenderness. The blade leads to the ear and takes with it the virtue conceived in the soul and draws it to the perfection of good deeds. Then the full grain comes to growth in the ear when virtue progresses to such a point that it produces hearty and perfect deeds." Obviously Olivi follows this line of interpretation. See Aquinas, *Catena Aurea*, 82-83 where he quotes Ps-Jerome, then Ps-Chrysostom, and finally Theophylactus. The latter (83) comments: "For we put forth the blade, when we show the principle of good; then the ear, when we can resist temptations; then comes the fruit, when a man works something perfect."

[32] Olivi seems to put into his own language what is found in Bede's Commentary on Mark. For his part, Bede is quoting Gregory's *Homilies on Ezekiel*. See CCSL, cxx, 486: "To produce the blade is the beginning of

"puts in the sickle" for the harvest. This also happens when a prelate most perfectly separates his perfect subjects from their own stubble. It also takes place when each individual, tossing away all chaff from his own full grain, most completely applies and disposes that full grain for the table of his own spiritual eating and tasting.

7) The fifth parable deals with the mustard seed growing into a tree.[33]

8) Mark 4:35-6:6. The sixth principal section, which deals with the confirmation by miracles of the teaching already given, presents four miracles. The first miracle highlights the calming of sea and wind.[34] The second concerns the cure of a demoniac possessed by a legion of demons.[35] The third and fourth miracles deal with the cure of a woman with a flow of blood and of the resuscitation of a little girl respectively.[36] After these miracles the text reads: "And leaving that place, he went into his own country."[37] It is indicated here why he performed merely a few miracles in Nazareth. He acted in this way not because of a defect in his power. Rather it was because of their lack of faith, occasioned by that familiarity that stems from having been raised together and from knowledge of who he was and who his parents were.[38]

---

doing good; this stage is characterized by tenderness. The blade leads to the ear and takes with it the virtue conceived in the soul and draws it to the perfection of good deeds. Then the full grain comes to growth in the ear when virtue progresses to such a point that it produces hearty and perfect deeds."

[33] See Mark 4:30-32.

[34] See Mark 4:35-40.

[35] See Mark 5:1-20.

[36] See Mark 5:21-43.

[37] See Mark 6:1.

[38] Is Olivi's comment a paraphrase of Bede's commentary, which he borrows from Jerome's commentary on Matthew? See CCSL cxx, 503: "… it is natural for citizens to be envious of their fellow citizens, for they do not consider the present deeds of a man, but remember his weak condition as an infant as if they, too, didn't progress through the same stages of growth to maturity."

9) Mark 6:7-33. The seventh principal section concerns the apostles' mission of preaching and begins in chapter 6 where the text states: "And he called the Twelve."[39] It has seven sub-sections. The first sub-section deals with the shape of this mission and has four components. The first is that they go on mission in pairs.[40] Second is the conferring of power over demons to restrict and expel them.[41] Third is the declaration of evangelical poverty.[42] Fourth is the shape and expression of the hospitality they receive.[43] The second sub-section mentions the Apostles' compliance with Christ's injunctions where the text reads: "And going forth, they preached ..."[44] The third sub-section focuses on the reputation that Christ's miracles have generated and that has reached Herod. There is also Herod's erroneous, but famous opinion of Jesus where the text states: "And King Herod heard of."[45] In the fourth sub-section the evangelist starts with Herod's opinion of Jesus and moves on to talk about John, whom Herod had previously imprisoned and beheaded. The text reads: "Herod

---

[39] See Mark 6:7.

[40] See Mark 6:7.

[41] See Mark 6:7.

[42] See Mark 6:8-9. Mark 6:8 plays a significant role in Olivi's argument about highest poverty. See Johannes Schlageter, *Das Heil der Armen und das Verderben der Reichen: Petrus Johannis Olivi OFM Die Frage nach der höchsten Armut*, Franziskanische Forschungen 34 (Werl/Westfalen: Dietrich-Coelde-Verlag, 1989), 104 and passim. See also what Olivi says about Luke 10:4 in *Petri Iohannis Olivi, Lectura super Lucam et Lectura super Marcum*, 398: "Fifth is the perfection of highest poverty where the text says: 'Do not carry a purse,' that is, a container for money or money bags of whatever sort, 'nor a bag,' that is, a container for bread or food.... From these words it is clear that Gregory understood that in the afore-mentioned evangelical poverty was the wondrous and highly edifying perfection of virtue." In contrast Albert the Great, *In Marcum*, 468 has a lengthy discussion about how Mark 6:8-9 relates to John 12:6 (Jesus' disciples have a money bag) and Luke 22:35-36 (there is a radical difference between the first sending and the present time of persecution). He writes: "... the Lord never prohibited in an absolute way the carrying of money. Rather he prohibited anxiety over money in situations where money was not necessary ..."

[43] See Mark 6:10-11.

[44] See Mark 6:12.

[45] See Mark 6:14.

himself had sent."[46] The fifth sub-section mentions the return
of the apostles where the text states: "And the apostles came
together."[47] The sixth sub-section presents Christ's leading
them aside to a quieter place where the text says: "And he
said to them: Come apart."[48] The seventh sub-section sets
forth the crowd's quick pursuit and anticipation of Christ's
and his disciples' destination where the text states: "And
they saw them."[49]

10) Mark 6:34-8:39. The eighth principal section commences in chapter 6 where the text has "And when he had
landed, Jesus saw a great crowd."[50] It deals with Christ's provident and marvelous rule and in twelve sub-sections wonder-
fully explains Christ's rule. The first sub-section presents the
superabundant feeding of five thousand with five loaves of
bread. The second sub-section sets forth the calming of the
stormy sea which had posed a grave threat to the disciples
who were navigating the boat where the text states: "And immediately afterwards he made his disciples."[51] The third sub-
section presents a summary account of his healing of many
infirm where the text has: "And crossing over, they came."[52]
The fourth sub-section concerns the nullifying or abolishing
of superstitious cleanliness and consequently the explication

---

[46] See Mark 6:14.
[47] See Mark 6:30.
[48] See Mark 6:31.
[49] See Mark 6:33.
[50] See Mark 6:34.
[51] See Mark 6:45. Olivi does not mention Jesus' walking on the water (6:48-49). Contrast what Albert the Great has in his *In Marcum*, 488:
"'Then he immediately spoke to them and said to them: It is I. Do not be
afraid. And he got into the boat with them, and the wind ceased.' Here is
the consolation of those who were afraid and the liberation of those who
were in danger. About their consolation the text says: 'Then immediately,'
the Lord, the consoler, 'spoke to them,' so that they might recognize by his
voice the one they had not known as he walked on the waves."
[52] See Mark 6:53-56: "... they came to land ... and they began to bring
the sick on their pallets, wherever they heard he was. And wherever he
went ... they laid the sick in the market places and entreated him to let
them touch but the tassel of his cloak. And as many as touched him were
saved."

and approbation of what truly and necessarily has to be observed where chapter 7 reads: "And the Pharisees and some of the scribes ... gathered about him."[53] The fifth sub-section deals with the avoidance of a person who is urging that it is a scandalous and failed approach to provide benefits to or associate with Gentiles and uneducated non-believers until their great faith in and devotion to God would demand another approach.[54] The text reads: "And he arose and departed from there for the district of Tyre."[55] The sixth sub-section presents the cure of the deaf-mute and the teaching and example to avoid vain glory contained in Jesus' command.[56] The text states: "And departing again from the district of Tyre."[57] Now the text continues: "He came to the Sea of Galilee through the midst of the district of the Decapolis,"[58] that is, as the Glossa comments: "to the place which is in the midst of the district of the Decapolis, that is, of the region of ten cities, which are a long distance beyond the Sea. It is not said that he had gone across the Sea, but to have come as far as the

---

[53] See Mark 7:1. The Vulgate reads *conveniunt* ("are gathering").

[54] See CCSL cxx, 434 where Bede's commentary gives this passage the following heading: ch. XXI: "He frees the daughter of the Syrophoenician woman from a demon." It seems that Albert the Great's interpretation sheds light on Olivi's exposition. See *In Marcum*, 503-04: "'For,' that is, since 'the dogs,' who are weak and cannot wait for the children to be filled, 'eat under the table.' While the sons are still being fed, the dogs eat of the tiniest 'crumbs of the children,' that is, of the sons. Thus, since I need to take care of my daughter, I cannot wait for the common feeding of the Gentiles, who are dogs. But take care of me right now while you are feeding the sons."

[55] See Mark 7:24-30 and the story of the Syrophoenician woman. See especially Mark 7:26: "Now the woman was a Gentile, a Syrophoenician by birth." Olivi does not mention the cure of the daughter of the Syrophoenician woman.

[56] See Aquinas, *Catena Aurea*, 143: "Pseudo-Chrys. He takes the deaf and dumb man who was brought to him apart from the crowd, that he might not do his divine miracles openly. He teaches us to cast away vain glory and swelling of heart ..."

[57] See Mark 7:31-37 and Jesus' command in 7:36: "And he charged them to tell no one."

[58] See Mark 7:31.

Sea, and therefore, he had not entered the district of the Decapolis which was beyond the Jordan to the east."[59]

11) But why "did he put his fingers into the ears" of the deaf man and "touch his tongue"[60] with his spittle?[61] The literal explanation is to show in a more evident manner that he was cured from his deafness and muteness by his power. But the mystical explanation is to prefigure the manner of the spiritual cure of sins symbolized by deafness and muteness. So he first took him "aside from the crowd,"[62] since while the din of earthly and worldly matters fills and occupies our mental hearing, we cannot obediently and delightfully listen to God's counsels and commandments or the canticles of God's praise. The fingers, distinct from each other and in which the sense of touch and the power of writing and working reside, signify the varied nature of divine forethought, by which God inscribes understanding and practical wisdom on our hearing. Through these we perform wisely the works of God. Another interpretation is that the fingers signify the different gifts of the Holy Spirit and the Spirit's spiritual senses.[63] In spittle resides the power to savor foods and to distinguish tastes, and by its temperate moistening the tongue becomes fit to speak. Thus it signifies the power of taste and the power to interpret the marvels of our God and of our faith. Among these marvels is the complete and integral confession of sins, through which God's justice and mercy flow.[64]

---

[59] See the Glossa Ordinaria on Mark 7:31 in PL 114:207B. See Collins, *Mark*, 369 for possible solutions for Mark's roundabout itinerary which is "like going from St. Louis to Dallas by way of Chicago and New York" (369 n. 54).

[60] See Mark 6:33.

[61] In n. 11-12 Olivi raises two questions to deepen his explanation of Mark 7:31-37 and in effect creates an excursus. See "Olivi's style of exegesis" in the Introduction.

[62] See Mark 6:33.

[63] See Bede's interpretation in CCSL cxx, 525: "He put his fingers into the ears since through the gifts of the Holy Spirit he opens the ears of the heart to understand and accept the words of salvation."

[64] See Albert the Great, *In Marcum*, 505-07: "... separation from the crowd signifies separation from the mass of perdition and from those who have perished. This is accomplished by taking hold of grace.... These fin-

12) Why "did he sigh"[65] while performing this cure? It must be said that by what he does once externally and sensibly, he wants us to understand what he was always doing internally. So while he was mortal, he was always suffering because of our sins and miseries and was petitioning the Father with deep sighs to provide a cure for them. Now he did not always manifest this, lest he seem unable to cure with power and authority.

13) The seventh sub-section[66] deals with the superabundant feeding of four thousand from seven loaves of bread where in chapter 8 it says: "In those days."[67] The eighth sub-section concerns the dispelling of those seeking empty signs where the text states: "And immediately getting into the boat."[68] The ninth sub-section sets forth Christ's motivation and formation of his disciples to more diligently understand and guard against the erroneous and hypocritical sect [of the Pharisees] and its teaching. With spiritual insight they are to assimilate his own way of life and teaching where the text reads: "And he left them and again got back into the boat."[69]

14) The tenth sub-section is the cure of a blind man which foretells what is to come. Also present here is the exempla-

---

gers signify the creative power by which he created all things through power, wisdom, and goodness.... And these are the first three fingers. Now the finger points to the power of the Holy Spirit through the gifts of wisdom and understanding, etc.... Spittle that descends from the head signifies the taste for divine things.... Here two ways of looking are mentioned. The first takes place with the eyes of the body and signifies that he refers all things to the Father in the harmony and unity he has with him. The other is of the heart which is signified by his sigh, by which he sighs on our behalf ..."

[65] See Mark 7:34.

[66] The sixth sub-section is found in n. 10-12.

[67] See Mark 8:1.

[68] See Mark 8:10. Mark 8:11 reads: "And the Pharisees came forth and began to dispute with him, demanding from him a sign from heaven to test him. And sighing deeply in spirit, he said: Why does this generation demand a sign? Amen I say to you: A sign will not be given to this generation."

[69] See Mark 8:13.

ry teaching about how to avoid vain glory when performing miracles of this kind. The text reads: "And they came to Bethsaida, and they brought him a blind man ... and he led him outside the village."[70] He does this for two reasons. First so that he might teach that one should flee from the vain glory of being popular in the public eye in these matters. That is why he takes some people away from the crowd and cures them. Second on account of the divine mystery treated earlier with regard to the deaf man.[71] The main reason is that the vanity of worldly society blinds the eyes of our heart, and therefore he has to lead us outside our village so that we might be enlightened.[72] "And applying spittle to his eyes, he laid his hands upon him,"[73] namely, upon the eyes of the blind man. "And he asked him if he saw anything."[74] Why did he not cure him right away and completely as he cured the others? Why is there a gradual change? The reason for this is twofold. The first is literal, so that he might show that there is not just one way of curing. Not only could he perform cures so that everything takes place in an instant, but he could also perform cures that take place successively. Otherwise he would not be completely free and able to act in various ways. He more frequently uses the way of the instantaneous cure because this more readily expresses his power. The second reason is mystical, and according to the Glossa one meaning is "that it may show the magnitude of human blindness which comes to light with effort and, as it were, by gradual steps. Also that it may indicate to us how he assists us by his

---

[70] See Mark 8:22-23.

[71] See n. 11 above.

[72] See Albert the Great, *In Marcum*, 525: "'He led him outside the village.' Second is the removal of the impediment to the cure, since in the tumult of the village where there is occasion of sin a person cannot be cured. In these villages and streets, that is, in the narrow and broad streets of concupiscence the spouse does not find God. Isaiah 43: 8 says: 'Bring forth the people that is blind.' Genesis 19:17 states: "Do not stay in all the country about, but save yourself on the mountain,' namely, away from humans who are sinners.'"

[73] See Mark 8:23.

[74] See Mark 8:23.

grace as we make progress in our perfection."[75] But this reason can be made more specific. By this miracle he showed the order and process of our knowledge, which is first confused and indistinct. Thus the text says that he first saw "human beings like trees,"[76] that is, according to the Glossa: "the form of bodies, so that it was impossible to easily discern whether they were human beings or trees."[77] Our second form of knowledge is clear and distinct. Wherefore, after Christ's second imposition of hands "he began to see,"[78] namely, plainly so that he saw everything clearly. Another interpretation is that by grace we are illumined to perceive the foolishness and shamefulness of human vanity, so that we might detest and flee from it. What is more foolish and shameful than that a human being, like an unfeeling tree, should have their feet and legs bent upwards like branches and to have their heads with their hair bent downwards like a root with its tendrils. Through the first vision Christ wanted to show us the dreadful foolishness of a human life that values fleshly things over spiritual things, temporal things over eternal things, and the lowest things over the highest things, and makes the supreme part of the soul fasten on to earthly feces. But by the other vision we are propelled by grace to see all things rightly and clearly. Another interpretation is that given by the Glossa: "Now the first steps along the way of virtue look closely at the life and moral behavior of others to imitate the good they do and to avoid the evil they do. A person who has been leading a life of foolishness does not immediately know how to discern between good and evil, faith and perfidy, sincerity and simulation. Light is given to that person by the second laying on of hands so that the person may discern matters of

---

[75] See the Glossa Ordinaria in PL 114:210D. This Glossa is based on Bede. See CCSL cxx, 534-35.

[76] See Mark 8:24.

[77] See *Biblia cum Glossa ordinaria et interlineari*, Volume IV, (Strasburg, 1481), ad loc. This Glossa is based on Bede. See CCSL cxx, 535.

[78] See Mark 8:25.

this kind and even discern all that is to be believed in and hoped for and fled from."[79]

15) The eleventh sub-section concerns Jesus' intimate question to his own: What do the people and you my disciples think of me? This is followed by Jesus' command that his disciples must keep silent about his majesty until the proper time. The text states: "And Jesus and his disciples entered."[80]

16) The twelfth and final sub-section deals with his clear prediction of his future passion and resurrection and his rousing exhortation to his disciples to embrace and accept this prediction where the text states: "And he began to teach them that the Son of Man must suffer."[81]

---

[79] See *Biblia cum Glossa ordinaria et interlineari*, Volume IV, (Strasburg, 1481), ad loc. The citation, based on Bede, is not verbatim. See CCSL cxx, 535. See also the exposition of Albert the Great, *In Marcum*, 524-27: "... 'that he might touch him,' firmly believing that with the touch of his hand, deity being united to this hand, he might bring about salvation. Job 5:18 states: 'He strikes, and his hands shall heal.' Just as they sought an outward touch, so too were they petitioning for the inward touch of compunction, realizing that unless sin is removed interiorly, the outside infirmity is not cured.... Psalm 143:5 says: 'Touch the mountains,' that is, the proud, 'and they will smoke.' ... 'He led him outside the village.' ... [Next] is the application of a taste for divine wisdom because saliva both descends from the head and has the taste of salt. It also signifies the gift of wisdom that descends from the head of the Christ of God and takes away the taste for sin by its taste.... 'Again he imposed his hands upon his eyes.' This second imposition of hands signifies the power of redeeming grace which came from Christ, for it removes from us all blindness. John 1:4-5 says: 'In him was life, and the life was the light of human beings. And the light shone in the darkness, and the darkness did not comprehend it.'"

[80] See Mark 8:27. It is obvious that Olivi makes no comment about Peter's confession. In contrast see Albert the Great, *In Marcum*, 527: "... there are three parts. The first one shows that the Church is founded by means of this divine power. The second shows that this divine power is perfected in grace through the weakness of the passion. See 8:34: 'And he began to teach them that the Son of Man,' etc. In the third he admonishes those founded on grace to follow along on the way of humility and patience. 8:34 states: 'And calling together the crowd with his disciples,' etc."

[81] See Mark 8:31.

17) Mark 9:1-29. In the ninth principal section which begins in chapter 9 with the words "And after six days"[82] the
evangelist treats the visible or experienced demonstration of
Christ's blessed glory and has three sub-sections. The first
presents the vision of Christ's glorious transfiguration whose
revelation is to be made after his resurrection. The second
sets forth the revelation of how Elijah, his precursor, has in
one way already come and in another way is still to come
where the text reads: "And they asked him, saying."[83] The
final presents the manifestation of his power over demons
in a miracle. Christ also tells his disciples that they could
obtain this power if they used the proper means where the
text states: "And on coming to his disciples, he saw a crowd,"
etc.[84]

18) Mark 9:30-10:52. The tenth principal section, which
begins later in chapter 9 with the words "Now he was teaching his disciples,"[85] concerns the perfection of Christ's counsels. These counsels are introduced by Christ's prediction of
his passion as the exemplar and causative perfection of all
the counsels. Then follows the evangelist's teaching about the
seven counsels or about difficult ways of perfection. The first
counsel is to engage in the most profound humility where
the text states: "And they came to Capernaum."[86] The second
counsel is the strong and diligent avoidance of giving scandal
to anyone at all and over anything at all and of the gracious
approbation and preservation of those things contributed by
anyone at all, even though they are non-believers.[87] The text

---

[82] See Mark 9:1.

[83] See Mark 9:10.

[84] See Mark 9:13. Olivi is referring to Mark 9:28: "And he said to them:
This kind can be cast out in no way except by prayer and fasting."

[85] See Mark 9:30.

[86] See Mark 9:32.

[87] Albert the Great may help explain Olivi's interpretation. See *In
Marcum*, 565: "'Who does not follow,' you whom we follow, by reason of
virtue and imitation of holiness, 'with us and we forbade him.' We wished
that whoever proclaims you is fit apostolically, both by reason of virtue
and from the sound teaching of the truth in word. But this would generate
great harm in the Church since many proclaim Christ in the Church, not

says: "John said to him: Master, we saw," etc.[88] The third counsel is the indissolubility, dependent on God alone, of chastity in whatever state a person is in. Mark 10 says: "And leaving that place"[89] where for the sake of brevity Mark omits what is said in Matthew 19 about the more expedient perfection of not marrying.[90] He presupposes these things from the sayings in Matthew and intimates that this is indicated in the indissolubility of a chaste marriage. Otherwise he would be placing it in a disharmonious manner among the counsels.[91] The fourth counsel deals with the special age that inaugurates the counsels of evangelical religion where the text reads: "And they were bringing little children to him."[92] This text indicates that the perfection of Christ's counsels is to be assumed as soon as possible after one has attained the first use of reason or after one has been converted to the faith. And in addition parents should tend to the greater perfection of their children by offering regular instructions and providing regular instructors. The fifth counsel is assent to highest and universal poverty where the text has: "And as he was going on a journey, a certain man ran up."[93] The sixth counsel is the embracing of Christ-formed martyrdom or suffering where the text states: "They were now on their way, going up

---

by reason of their life, but rather because of their good deeds. Thus Philippians 1:17 states: 'Some proclaim Christ out of contentiousness and not sincerely...' A little later verse 18 says: 'But what of it? Provided only that in every way, whether in pretense or in truth, Christ is being proclaimed. In this I rejoice. Yes, and I will rejoice.' And so Christ corrects this error in the Apostles."

[88] See Mark 9:37.

[89] See Mark 10:1.

[90] See Matt 19:10-12.

[91] See Collins, *Mark*, 468-69 for possible contemporary solutions to the differences between Mark 10:1-12 and Matt 19:1-12. See 469: "Mark 10:2-9 could, then, have arisen in order to discourage divorce for the sake of some ideal in tension with marriage, whether it be sexual self-mastery or dedication to the itinerant proclamation of the gospel."

[92] See Mark 10:13.

[93] See Mark 10:17-31. See Albert the Great, *In Marcum*, 597-98 where he deals with contrary opinions why the youth was sad (v. 22) and concludes on 598: "But he was sad about giving away all his possessions and about begging. And this is not contrary to salvation, but to perfection according to the state of the greatest poverty."

to Jerusalem."[94] Here Christ is portrayed as admirably going on ahead to his passion. To those who are dearest to him on the way he gives counsel and charges them as the text states: "And James and John came to him."[95] And therefore, because of this situation he again adds the counsel of evangelical humiliation, even until death, where the text says: "And when the ten heard this."[96] When the text says "Jesus was walking in front of them and they were bewildered and those who followed were afraid,"[97] the sense is this. Knowing the horrendous anger and implacable hatred of the Jews towards Christ, they were afraid to follow him into Jerusalem and were amazed that he was going there with such eagerness, especially since he was saying that he was to be crucified there. They did not fully understand what he was saying and thought that he was speaking in parables.[98] The seventh counsel is indefectible, faithful, and persistent prayer that always grows in strength and constancy.[99] The power and approbation of this prayer are actually taught in the miracle

---

[94] See Mark 10:32.

[95] See Mark 10:35.

[96] See Mark 10:41.

[97] See Mark 10:32.

[98] For a different interpretation see Albert the Great, *In Marcum*, 607: "'and Jesus was going on ahead of them.' Just as he was going ahead of them on the road, so too was he going ahead of them in the perfection of a totally good life. Micah 2:13 says: 'The one that will open the way before them will go up.' Isa 45:2 states: 'I will go before you, and will humiliate the great ones of the earth.' Ps 18:6 has: 'He has rejoiced as a giant to run the way.' Hebr 12:1-2 reads: 'Let us run to the fight set before us, looking towards the author and finisher of faith, Jesus, who for the joy set before him, endured a cross, despising shame, and sits at the right hand of the throne of God.' 1 Cor 4:16 says: 'Be imitators of me, as I am of Christ.' 'And they were bewildered' by the words of his wisdom. Luke 5:9 states: 'Stupor enveloped Peter and all who were with him.' 'And they were afraid,' lest they be cut off from such a height of perfection. Hebr 2:1 has: 'Therefore, we ought the more earnestly observe the things that we have heard, lest perhaps we drift away.' Rom 11:20 reads: 'Be not high-minded, but fear.'"

[99] See Albert the Great, *In Marcum*, 616: "'But he cried out all the louder: Son of David, have mercy on me.' Here is insistent petitioning, and there are three things that add to the insistence, namely, the rebuke of the bystanders, who could not stop this man from crying out; the man's continuous crying out; the repetition of the man's plea."

story of a blind man where the text reads: "And they came to Jericho."[100]

19) Mark 11:1-33. The eleventh principal section begins in the eleventh chapter where it says "and when Jesus drew near to Jerusalem."[101] This section deals with the royal honor of Christ and touches upon and proclaims his royal or overwhelmingly dominant power in seven sub-sections. The first presents the loosing and bringing of the colt, authorized by his command, and his sitting upon it. The second sets forth the deferential and joyful honor the crowd pays him where the text reads: "Many spread their cloaks."[102] The third presents the unfailing amazement at his royal dignity which didn't try to flatter anyone where the text has: "And he entered Jerusalem."[103] The fourth presents the cursing and withering up of the fig tree as a type of Jewish sterility and wickedness where the text reads: "And the next day he went out."[104] The fifth sets forth the astonishing expulsion of those doing business in the temple where the text says: "And when he had entered the Temple."[105] The sixth sets forth the disciples' recognition on the next day that the fig tree had withered up because of his miracle. On this same occasion the obtaining and performing of miracles of whatever type and even the obtaining of all gifts are promised to those who have solid faith and engage in faithful and devout prayer where the text reads: "And when it was evening."[106] The seventh presents the triumphal confounding of the Jews who wished to weaken Christ's dominant and corrective power by

---

[100] See Mark 10:46.
[101] See Mark 11:1.
[102] See Mark 11:8.
[103] See Mark 11:11. Olivi's point seems to be the contrast between Christ's "triumphal" entry into Jerusalem (11:1-10) and his non-reception in Jerusalem as hinted at by 11:11: "And he went into Jerusalem, into the Temple. And when he had looked round upon all things, then, as it was already late, he went out to Bethany with the Twelve."
[104] See Mark 11:12.
[105] See Mark 11:15.
[106] See Mark 11:19.

their questioning where the text states: "And they went back to Jerusalem."[107]

20) Note that the expulsion of the sellers, which occurs in this chapter, seems to have taken place on the Monday after Palm Sunday.[108] The reason is that Mark says that "when it was evening,"[109] namely, of the aforementioned day of the expulsion "he went out of the city," namely, to go to Bethany. The text continues: "when they passed by on [the following] morning,"[110] that is, they were returning from Bethany to Jerusalem, the disciples saw "the fig tree withered up," which Christ on the preceding day, namely, Monday, had cursed and caused to wither, as has been stated above. Now from these considerations it seems to necessarily follow that the expulsion of the sellers took place on Monday. Therefore, either he expelled them twice, namely, on Palm Sunday and again on the following day, or when Matthew[111] and Luke[112] refer to the expulsion as if it were performed on Palm Sunday, they must be referring to the following day. Now what Mark says, namely, "and when he had entered the Temple, he began to expel the sellers,"[113] could be said by means of recapitulation or in reverse order with respect to what immediately preceded it, namely, "and they came to Jerusalem,"[114] referring to his entry which occurred on "the next day"[115] after Palm Sunday. However, what the text adds, namely, "and when it was evening,"[116] can only mean the evening of that day when the expulsion of the sellers took place. This problem cannot

---

[107] See Mark 11:27.

[108] See "Olivi's style of exegesis" in the Introduction for Olivi's use of the imperatival "note," which functions here almost as an excursus on the dating of Christ's expulsion of the sellers from the Temple.

[109] See Mark 11:19.

[110] See Mark 11:20.

[111] See Matt 21:12-17.

[112] See Luke 19:45-48. Luke does not recount Jesus' cursing of the fig tree and its withering up.

[113] See Mark 11:15.

[114] See Mark 11:11.

[115] See Mark 11:12.

[116] See Mark 11:19.

be solved by referring to what the Master of the Histories maintains, namely, that the fig tree had been cursed on Palm Sunday when Christ entered the city.[117] The reason is that it is said in Matthew 21 that, after Christ had entered the Temple, the high priests had said: "Do you hear what these [children] are saying?" and he had said to them: "Yes ... because out of the mouth of infants ..." which indeed took place on Palm Sunday.[118] Matthew 21 continues: "Leaving them, he went out to Bethany"[119] and "in the morning on his way back"[120] he cursed the fig tree. From this it necessarily follows that he cursed the fig tree not on Sunday, but on Monday. Now after Christ's cursing of the fig tree Matthew adds: "and when he had come into the Temple," namely, on Monday, "the chief priests" said to him: "By what authority are you doing these things?"[121] The words, "these things," refer to the expulsion of the sellers from the Temple. So from Matthew it is sufficiently clear that Christ had performed the expulsion at that time, because it is likely that the chief priests would have said this to him immediately after he had expelled the sellers or while he was expelling them. Further, Mark, having said that Jesus entered the Temple on Palm Sunday, adds that "when he had looked around at all things, and since it was evening, he went out to Bethany ... and on the next day, after they had left Bethany, he was hungry"[122] and he cursed the fig tree. Although one could possibly read the Latin *alia die* to refer to the preceding day, the literal meaning is more clear and the words should be read as "and on the next day." Further, the aforementioned quotations from Matthew compel us that this is the necessary interpretation. Moreover, if *alia die* were taken to mean the preceding day, then the cursing of the fig tree would have taken place on the Sabbath

---

[117] See ch. 117 of Peter Comestor, *Historia scholastica* in PL 198:1599B.

[118] See Matt 21:16.

[119] See Matt 21:16.

[120] See Matt 21:18.

[121] See Matt 21:23.

[122] See Mark 11:11-12.

before Palm Sunday. But no one is of this opinion, and it is even against the position of the Master cited earlier.[123]

21) Mark 12:1-13:37. In the twelfth principal section, which begins in chapter 12 with the words "And he began to speak,"[124] there are seven sub-sections that pertain to Christ's judgment. The first sets forth the just ruin of the Jews as the perverse workers of the vineyard of the Lord and the introduction of other workers to care for the vineyard.[125] The second presents the unassailable declaration to render to God and to the earthly ruler what pertains to them, where the text reads: "And they sent to him."[126] The third sets forth instruction about the future resurrection and its most chaste incorruption, where the text states: "And Sadducees came to him."[127] The fourth sets forth the two principal commandments for meriting and obtaining the kingdom of God where

---

[123] Collins, *Mark*, 526-32 does not deal with the dating of Jesus' expulsion of the sellers from the Temple as a historical critical problem worthy of note.

[124] See Mark 12:1.

[125] See Mark 12:1-12. See Wailes, *Medieval Allegories*, 152: "In the thirteenth century it is less common to explain this parable with the vineyard as the Jewish people than with a formulation stressing the spiritual endowment." Spiritual endowment means that through baptism each Christian receives a vine and must tend it. See Albert the Great, *In Marcum*, 643-49 where he provides a good example of "the spiritual endowment" interpretation. For example, on 648 he interprets Mark 12:8 in this way: "This, too, we do as often as we reject and trample underfoot Christ's grace offered to us and toss it outside the vineyard of our hearts in which virtues should be planted that will bring forth joy."

[126] See Mark 12:13-17.

[127] See Mark 12:18-27, esp. v. 25: "For when they rise from the dead, they will neither marry nor be given in marriage, but are as angels in heaven." See Albert the Great, *In Marcum*, 655: "But there all fecundity comes from the joining together of a created spirit with the uncreated one. 'But they will be.' Here he touches on the teaching of truth. 'But they will be' in the future 'like angels,' not in the nature of an angel, but like angels in their property of being spiritual and immortal. And since marriage is a good of mortals, therefore there is no marrying or giving in marriage.... Thus the Glossa states: 'No one dies there; no one is born there; there is no infant or old person there.'"

the text states: "And one of the scribes came forward."[128] The fifth presents the proof given by the Psalmist for Christ's power to judge as co-ruler with God the Father where the text has: "While Jesus was teaching in the Temple, he asked: So how ...?"[129] The sixth sets forth the awesome and grave weighing at Christ's final judgment of the hypocritical sinners and their showy gifts. His judgment is against the superficial appearance and smallness of their gifts and works, where the text states: "And in the course of his teaching, he said to them: Beware of the scribes."[130] The seventh sub-section presents the most complete explanation of the judgment against the synagogue and finally of the entire world as well as their signs where it says in chapter 13: "And as he was going out of the Temple."[131]

22) This seventh sub-section has a further seven sections. First is the prediction of the total destruction of the Jewish Temple. Second is the private questioning of Christ as to the time and the signs of the final judgment where the text reads: "And as he was sitting on the Mount of Olives."[132] Third is Christ's teaching of the four things that come before and initiate the final judgment, namely, the arrival of many very seductive anti-Christs[133] and false prophets and

---

[128] See Mark 12:28-34. Olivi does not mention that "one of the Scribes" appears in a positive light in Mark 12:28-34. See, e.g., Mark 12:34: "And Jesus, seeing that he had answered wisely, said to him: You are not far from the kingdom of God."

[129] See Mark 12:35-37, esp. v. 35: "And while Jesus was teaching in the Temple, he addressed them, asking: How do the scribes say that the Christ is the Son of God?" See Albert the Great, *In Marcum*, 662: "'At my right hand,' that is, in total equality of power.... 'Until I make'... This is the time that goes along until the day of judgment. During all of this time enemies are being subjected to Christ."

[130] See Mark 12:38. It seems strange that Olivi, a champion of poverty, does not comment specifically on the "widow's mite" and the widow's poverty in Mark 12:41-44.

[131] See Mark 13:1.

[132] See Mark 13:3.

[133] The Vulgate reads *pseudochristi* ("false Christs") at Mark 13:22. Albert the Great also interprets "false christs" as anti-Christs. See *In Marcum*, 678: "In that time, 'false christs,' who will truly be anti-Christs [will

the rumors of wars and the reckoning or dread of their calamities as well as varied and unaccustomed earthquakes and the poverty of famine where the text says: "And Jesus responded."[134] In the fourth he says that before the things predicted take place, all the Gentiles must be evangelized by the apostles and the faithful who will endure many beatings. He comforts them and encourages them to be steadfast and to persevere where the text has: "Watch out for yourselves."[135] The fifth shows more fully the extent of the tribulations from the anti-Christ[136] where the text says: "And when you see."[137] The sixth presents the teaching concerning the future judgment after that tribulation and what its signs are where the text states: "But in those days."[138] The seventh sets forth the teaching concerning the secret nature of the day or hour of that judgment which forces us to be vigilant for that day and to be always prepared. The text reads: "But of that day or hour."[139]

PART II: CHRIST'S PASSION AND DEATH[140]

23) "And it was Passover."[141] Having completed the first part of his book, which deals with the course of Christ's preaching, the evangelist now turns to his passion and death. This part has four principal sections. The first shows: the wickedness of those who procure his capture and death; Christ's ardent

---

arise], but they will be lying that they are Christ. 1 John 2:18 states: 'Many anti-Christs have arisen.' And 1 John 4:3 says: 'Every spirit that severs Jesus is not of God, but is of the anti-Christ of whom you have heard that he is coming.'"

[134] See Mark 13:5.

[135] See Mark 13:9.

[136] Mark 13 does not refer to an "anti-Christ," but to "false Christs." See Mark 13:22. Space does not allow Olivi the opportunity to comment about the anti-Christs. See his *Commentary on Revelation*.

[137] See Mark 13:14.

[138] See Mark 13:24.

[139] See Mark 13:32.

[140] Mark 14:1-15:47.

[141] See Mark 14:1.

and prescient love to undergo his death; the weakness of the disciples. The second sets forth the horrendous and violent tumult attendant to his capture and condemnation where the text reads: "And while he was still speaking."[142] The third presents the ignominy of his crucifixion relative to those crucified, but the glorious wonder relative to the divine signs where chapter 15 below states: "And after they had mocked him."[143] The fourth displays the prompt obedience of some of his devoted followers to provide assistance and to bury him where the text says: "Now there were also women."[144]

24) Mark 14:1-42. In the first principal section there are seven sub-sections. The first sets forth the traitorous procuring of Christ's capture and death. The motivating cause and reason for this wickedness was the horrendous cupidity violently launched against Mary for wasting precious ointment on Christ.[145] So when this event is remembered, what Mary had done will be recalled. Mary's anointing of Jesus before his death is commemorated on this occasion. The procuring of this betrayal was accomplished on the Wednesday after Palm Sunday. Wherefore, it is said here that it was "Passover," that is, the immolation of the paschal lamb, "and unleavened bread," that is, the celebration of Unleavened Bread,

---

[142] See Mark 14:43.

[143] See Mark 15:1.

[144] See Mark 15:40.

[145] Mark's account of the anointing in 14:3-9 does not name the woman. See John 12:1-11 which mentions Mary as the one who anointed Jesus. Olivi seems dependent on Bede, CCSL cxx, 607, who observes that Mark is indebted to John 12:6 here and makes the special point that the motivating factor for Judas's criticism of the anointing was cupidity. Albert the Great, *In Marcum*, 691 also introduces the element of cupidity: "'and given to the poor.' Note the hypocrisy here since under the species of piety he hides his avarice and gives birth to betrayal. He did not care for the poor or try to help them. Rather through this statement he wants to cover his avarice and to incite the indignation of the disciples against Christ and the pious woman. John 12:6 says: 'Now he said this, not because he cared for the poor, but because he was a thief, and holding the money bag, used to take what was put into it,' that is, he used to carry it off and steal it. Job 27:8 states: 'For what is the hope of the hypocrite if through avarice he violently takes something and God does not free his soul?'"

which was "two days away."[146] Now Mary did what she did on the preceding Sabbath. The text also adds the attempt by and desire of the high priests against Christ "by stealth,"[147] that is, to seize him by some fraudulent and traitorous way. The text also shows how both they and Judas were traitors and how easily and quickly Judas could procure this betrayal with them since he had already agreed with their desire and attempt to seize him.

25) The second sub-section presents Christ's celebration of the paschal lamb with his own where the text states: "On the first day of the Unleavened Bread."[148] This is the fourteenth lunar day which then was Thursday. It was called the day of Unleavened Bread by synecdoche because late that day or in the evening the festival of the Unleavened Bread began. At other times the following day was properly called the first day of Unleavened Bread, although it began on the evening of the preceding day. According to the reckoning behind these obligatory festivals, they were considered to begin on the following day. However, according to the flow of nature and sensible appearances[149] they were considered to begin on the preceding day.[150] Mark follows this latter practice.[151]

---

[146] See Mark 14:1: "Now it was two days before the Passover and the feast of the Unleavened Bread. The chief priests and the scribes were seeking how they might seize him by stealth and put him to death."

[147] See Mark 14:1.

[148] See Mark 14:12.

[149] It seems that Olivi is referring to sunset as the end of a day.

[150] Implied is the question of when a day begins. In Jewish calculations a day begins at sunset. Olivi seems to think that a liturgical day began at midnight whereas popular parlance considered a day to begin at sunset.

[151] See Collins, *Mark*, 640. R.T. France's historical critical commentary is more expansive. See R.T. France, *The Gospel of Mark: A Commentary on the Greek Text*, The New International Greek Testament Commentary (Grand Rapids: Eerdmans, 2002), 548: "The Passover proper therefore spanned Nisan 14 and 15. The festival of Unleavened Bread ... originally a separate festival, followed on directly from the Passover and lasted seven days.... In practice the two festivals were treated together as a single period of celebration ..."

26) The third sub-section treats Christ's prediction that one of the Twelve was going to betray him where the text has: "Jesus said: I say to you that one of you."[152]

27) The fourth sub-section presents the tradition of the sacramental celebration of his body and blood in memory of his passion. It also sets forth the prediction that Christ would not eat or drink anything else until after his resurrection where the text states: "And while they were eating."[153]

28) The fifth sub-section presents Christ's leading his disciples forth to the place of his capture and his prediction that his disciples would be scandalized and fall on account of his passion. There is also a more specific prediction of Peter's threefold denial where the text reads: "And after reciting a hymn."[154]

29) The sixth sub-section presents Christ's prayer of petition to the Father about the death that would be horrific and would naturally fill him with dread. He also presents his obedient subjection, compliance, and conformity to the Father's will. Along with this is his exhortation to his disciples to be vigilant in prayer and their great weakness and sluggishness in the light of these things where the text says: "And he said to his disciples: Sit down here while I pray."[155] At the end he said to them: "Sleep now and take your rest. It is enough."[156] These words can be understood to mean that he had said this as allowing them a modicum of sleep because they were weighed down with sleep. After they had slept a while, he said to them: "it is enough," namely, you have slept until now. Now the hour of my arrest is at hand. Augustine in his *Harmony of the Gospels* follows this man-

---

[152] See Mark 14:18.
[153] See Mark 14:22.
[154] See Mark 14:26.
[155] See Mark 14:32.
[156] See Mark 14:41.

ner of interpretation.[157] Another interpretation is that these words could be understood as irony, as if he were saying: Is now the time for sleeping? And then against this sleeping he adds: "It is enough" that you have been filled with torpor until now, for now the time of my passion is here, and you must be vigilant.[158] A third interpretation is possible: It is not necessary to pray now for his liberation from arrest and death, for their fulfillment is now at hand. The sense then is this: "Sleep now," since it is not necessary now to pray. "It is sufficient" to have prayed until this time in this manner, but now "is the hour" of his arrest.[159]

30) The seventh sub-section presents Christ's alacrity in going to meet those who have come to arrest him and his rousing encouragement that his disciples join in where the text states: "Rise, let us go."[160]

31) Mark 14:43-15:19. Likewise there are seven sub-sections in the second principal section which begins with "And while he was still speaking."[161] It sets forth the horrendous

---

[157] See Book III, ch. 4 in CSEL xliii, 283. See also NPNF, Series 1, Volume 6, 182-83.

[158] See *Catena Aurea*, 296: "And that he spoke ironically is evident, by what is added: *It is enough, the hour is come; behold, the Son of man is betrayed into the hands of sinners.* He speaks this, as deriding their sleep, as if he had said: Now indeed is a time for sleep, when the traitor is approaching." See Collins, *Mark*, 682: "When Jesus comes the third time, he says: 'Sleep now, and rest; it is enough' (v. 41b). This remark appears to be in tension with the command and exhortation in v. 42a, 'Get up; let us go.' This tension signifies at least for the text in its Markan form, that the remark 'Sleep now and rest' is ironic, perhaps even sarcastic. Jesus is portrayed as exasperated and realizes that 'it is enough,' that is, that he has been unsuccessful in exhorting the disciples to keep awake."

[159] See Albert the Great, *In Marcum*, 710-11: "He said this so that his disciples, refreshed by sleep, could flee from the hands of those who were about to seize Christ. Job 3:17 states: 'Those who have been sapped of strength have rested.' Qoheleth 5:11 says: 'Sleep is sweet to a laborer, whether he eats little or much.' And after they had rested, he said to them 'it is enough,' that you have rest to this extent. 'The hour has come' for me to be handed over and for you to flee."

[160] See Mark 14:42.

[161] See Mark 14:43.

tumult attendant to his arrest and the judgment against him. The first sub-section highlights his tumultuous and traitorous capture. The second presents his abandonment by his disciples where the text states: "Then his disciples."[162] In the third sub-section Christ is led to the high priest, questioned, condemned, and mocked where the text reads: "And they led Jesus away."[163] Into this sequence of events the evangelist inserts how "Peter followed him ... to the courtyard of the high priest."[164] The fourth sub-section sets forth Peter's threefold denial caused by terror at such a great and violent commotion where the text says: "And while Peter was below."[165] The fifth sub-section presents the leading of Christ to Pilate and Pilate's examination of him where chapter 15 has: "And as soon as it was morning."[166] The sixth sub-section sets forth Pilate's intention to free Christ and his many attempts to do so which were countered repeatedly by the Jews where the text states: "Now at festival time."[167] The seventh sub-section presents Pilate's handing over of Christ to death, mockery, and flagellation as if he were compelled to do so by the Jews where the text says: "Now Pilate, wishing to satisfy the people."[168]

32) Mark 15:20-39. The third principal section commences with "And after they had mocked him"[169] and deals with his crucifixion. It consists of nine sub-sections. The first sub-section narrates how he was led to the place of crucifixion

---

[162] See Mark 14:50: "Then all his disciples left him and fled."

[163] See Mark 14:53-65.

[164] See Mark 14:54.

[165] See Mark 14:66. Olivi seems to lessen the denial of Peter. Contrast Albert the Great, *In Marcum*, 722: "Peter's threefold denial is that he denies knowledge, he renounces Christ and his discipleship, and he denies eternal truth with an oath." Earlier, on 722, Albert the Great observed: "If the one, whom God constituted as the leader and foundation of the Church, denied [Christ] because of the voice of a handmaid, what are you going to do when you fall into a similar temptation?"

[166] See Mark 15:1.

[167] See Mark 15:6.

[168] See Mark 15:15.

[169] See Mark 15:20.

and how he carried his cross after him. The second deals with his crucifixion and the dividing of his garments where the text has: "And they crucified him."[170] The third sets forth the inscription of the title that stated the reason for his triumphal death where the text states: "And the inscription."[171] The fourth presents the crucifixion of two thieves alongside him which adds to his ignominy where the text reads: "And they crucified with him."[172] The fifth presents the derisory blasphemy and scorning of the crucified Christ by passers-by, the high priests, scribes, and even the thieves where the text says: "And the passers-by," that is, travelers, "blasphemed him."[173] The sixth sets forth the darkness over the whole land for three hours or according to some for three and a half hours where the text states: "And when the sixth hour came."[174] The seventh sets forth Christ's amazing cry about the ninth hour to God where the text reads: "And at the ninth hour."[175] The eighth presents the false judgment of some about this event which resulted in the offer of a bitter drink to Christ where the text has: "And some of the bystanders."[176] The ninth sets forth Christ's expiration by means of the miracle of a loud voice and the centurion's proclamation, made because of this miracle, that he was truly the Son of God.[177] This miracle

---

[170] See Mark 15:24.

[171] See Mark 15:26. See Albert the Great, *In Marcum*, 736: "Triumphal is this title, on which Christ triumphed over death and the author of death. He broke open the prison of death and liberated his own. Isa 63:1 states: 'I speak of justice and am a defender who saves.' Hosea 13:14 says: 'I will be your death, O Death. O Hell, I will sting you.'"

[172] See Mark 15:27.

[173] See Mark 15:29.

[174] See Mark 15:33.

[175] See Mark 15:34.

[176] See Mark 15:35-36.

[177] See Bede's comment on Mark 15:39 in CCSL cxx, 636: "The obvious reason for the miracle of the centurion is this: Seeing that the Lord had expired in this way, that is, to have sent forth his spirit, he said: Truly this man was the Son of God. No one has the power to send forth the spirit unless he is the one who created souls." Bede is quoting from Jerome's commentary on Matthew in PL 26:222. See also *First Commentary on Mark*, 123: "We die with a low cry or without any, because we are of the earth. However, he dies with a raised cry because he has come down from heaven." See further Albert the Great, *In Marcum*, 741: "'And Jesus':

was augmented by the complete rending of the Temple curtain before the Holy of Holies where the text says: "But Jesus cried out with a loud voice."[178]

33) Mark 15:40-47. The fourth principal section begins with "Now there were also women there."[179] It presents the devotion and service of some women to Christ and has two sub-sections. The first sets forth the devout assistance certain ladies gave him on the cross. The second one presents Joseph's reverent homage in asking Pilate for Christ's body and honoring it with burial where the text states: "And when it was evening."[180]

PART III: CHRIST'S RESURRECTION AND ASCENSION[181]

34) "Now Mary Magdalene."[182] Now that the second part of his book has been completed, which dealt with Christ's passion, the evangelist adds the third and final part which sets forth his glorious resurrection, appearances, and ascension. There actually is a threefold apparition of the resurrected one and then his ascension into heaven. After that the apostolic preaching to the entire world is mentioned. It is a preaching confirmed sufficiently by miracles. The principal

---

Intent on the work of our redemption, not on the insults of those taunting him, 'crying out with a loud voice,' which indicated that he still had great power, 'died,' that is, handed over his spirit into the hands of the Father. Luke 23:46 reads: 'Father, into your hands I commend my spirit.' John 19:30 has: 'When he had taken the wine, he said: It is consummated. And bowing his head, he gave up his spirit.'" See *Catena Aurea*, 326-27: "We who are of the earth die with a very low voice, or with no voice at all; but he who descended from heaven breathed his last with a loud voice.... But seeing that he died with such power as the Lord, he (the centurion) wondered and confessed."

[178] See Mark 15:37-38.
[179] See Mark 15:40.
[180] See Mark 15:42.
[181] Mark 16:1-20.
[182] See Mark 16:1.

sections are clear. The narration of his second appearance begins with "And after this to two."[183] The third appearance is narrated where the text reads: "Finally."[184] The ascension is found at "So then the Lord Jesus."[185] Mention of the preaching occurs where the text states: "But they went forth."[186] This event is added here according to a literal reason. That is, it shows how the disciples' preaching fulfilled what Christ had commanded and promised them in his third appearance.

35) Mark 16:1-11. In the first principal section the first sub-section shows the devotion of Mary Magdalene with the rest of the ladies in coming to anoint Christ. This devotion in some way merits their vision. The second sub-section sets forth the angelic appearance and announcement, further disposing them to these events where the text states: "And on entering the tomb."[187] The third sub-section presents Christ's primordial appearance to Magdalene where the text reads: "When he had risen from the tomb early."[188] The fourth sub-section sets forth her announcement to the disciples that she had seen him and their obduracy in not believing where the text says: "She went."[189]

36) Mark 16:12-13. In the second principal section the second vision occurs. It begins with the words "After this."[190] It has two brief sub-sections. The first sets forth the vision

---

[183] See Mark 16:12. Mark 16:9 indicates that Christ first appeared to Mary Magdalene.

[184] See Mark 16:14.

[185] See Mark 16:19.

[186] See Mark 16:20.

[187] See Mark 16:5.

[188] See Mark 16:9. Contrast what Albert the Great, *In Marcum*, 755 says: "'First he appeared to Mary Magdalene.' That is, among those through whom he proved his resurrection, since he appeared to his Mother, the Blessed Virgin Mary, first of all, not to prove his resurrection, but to make her heart rejoice in seeing him. But through Mary Magdalene he proved his resurrection. And the text says why he appeared to her first of all: 'Out of whom he had cast out seven demons.' Rom 5:20 says: 'Where the offense has abounded, grace has abounded more'..."

[189] See Mark 16:10-11.

[190] See Mark 16:12.

given to two people. The second states that they announce this to others who are obdurate in not believing where the text has: "And they went."[191] It is not to be understood that all were incredulous in this matter. Indeed, some of them were, since Luke says that when these two returned to the others, they were saying that "the Lord had truly risen and has appeared to Simon,"[192] and then the two of them began to narrate how they had seen him.

37) Mark 16:14-20. In the third principal section which begins with "Finally he appeared"[193] the first sub-section presents Christ's appearance to the disciples and his rebuke of them for their incredulity. The second sub-section sets forth his sending them forth to preach to the entire world, which is to be understood to take place not immediately, but at its proper time which he will reveal to them where the text states: "And he said to them."[194] The third sub-section mentions the reward for believers and the condemnation for unbelievers where the text says: "Whoever believes."[195] The fourth sub-section is the gift to the faithful of the power to work miracles where the text has: "And signs."[196]

38) Note[197] that according to Augustine in his *Harmony of the Gospels*, although this appearance could be taken as the last of those that occurred on the first day of resurrection, it is more likely that it was simply the last of all those appearances made to the Eleven "while they were at table" or eating together. After that appearance followed the one when they saw Christ ascending into heaven, which is narrated in Acts 1.[198] It is not contrary to this opinion that Christ is

---

[191] See Mark 16:13.

[192] See Luke 24:34.

[193] See Mark 16:14.

[194] See Mark 16:15.

[195] See Mark 16:16.

[196] See Mark 16:17.

[197] See "Olivi's style of exegesis" in the Introduction for Olivi's use of the imperatival "note."

[198] Cf. Book III, ch. 25 n. 76 in CSEL xliii, 379-80 and NPNF 1, Volume 6, 220. Olivi gives the gist of Augustine's argument. The reference is to

said to "have upbraided them for their hardness of heart and incredulity,"[199] since this can be understood in two ways.[200] In the first understanding the words "upbraided them for their incredulity" refer to the past, not the present, because earlier they were exceedingly obdurate and slow to believe. Indeed this upbraiding was useful both for them and for us. It was useful for them, so that they might mourn more deeply over their prior slowness in coming to belief and that it might inflame and inspire them more deeply to pursue the opposite. For us they provide an example and teaching to avoid similar slowness and more quickly and strongly come to and persist in faith in divine things. The second interpretation is to take the words "to upbraid their incredulity" to refer not to all of the disciples, but only to those who up until now had not completely believed. Wherefore, he also distinguishes here between some who had seen and others who had not believed those who had seen.

39) Furthermore, note[201] that the expression "signs shall attend those who believe," etc.[202] is, according to the literal sense, to be understood of those who perfectly believe and to apply to signs that are necessary or very expedient in confirming the faith.[203] However, mystically this expression can

---

Acts 1:9-11. Is Olivi actually citing Augustine or is he here citing Bede who quotes Augustine. See CCSL cxx, 644. See Albert the Great, *In Marcum*, 736: "So the text says 'lastly,' not with regard to the number of the apparitions, but in accordance with the order of the days since this apparition, which took place on the fortieth day from the Resurrection, occurred in the morning in Jerusalem in the upper room. After this day there were no more appearances." See Collins, *Mark*, 808-09 who does not address this historical critical question because she is focused on the sources and interrelationships of the various endings of Mark's Gospel. See also France, *Mark*, who doesn't even include the endings of Mark 16:9-20 in his commentary. For him Mark's Gospel ended with Mark 16:8.

[199] See Mark 16:14.

[200] See Collins, *Mark*, 808-09 for a different resolution of this issue.

[201] This is a further instance of Olivi's use of the imperatival "note." See also n. 20 and 38 above.

[202] See Mark 16:17.

[203] See Albert the Great, *In Marcum*, 758: "[These signs] are the fruit of those who preach faithfully and are believers. And he says that there are

be understood of the expulsion of sins and the newness of doctrinal and spiritual sermons which continually happen in the Church through the faithful and ecclesiastical sacraments, as Gregory explains in his homily on the Feast of the Ascension.[204]

---

five, whose literal meaning is clear as they are interpreted singly. Indeed he gives an advance summary of them: 'Signs will attend those who believe,' on account of the merit of their faith. John 13:12 [14:12] states: 'the person who believes in me, the works that I do, he also will do, and greater than these he will do, because I am going to the Father.' 'Will attend' their preaching. Hebr 2:4 says: 'God bearing them witness by signs and wonders and manifest powers ...'"

[204] See Homily 29 in *Gregorius Magnvs, Homilia in Evangelia*, edited by Raymond Étaix, CCSL cxli (Turnhout: Brepols, 1999), 247-49. See also *Gregory the Great: Forty Gospel Homilies*, translated from the Latin by David Hurst, Cistercian Study Series 123 (Kalamazoo, Michigan: Cistercian Publications, 1990), 227: "When its priests impose their hands on believers through the gift of exorcism and forbid the evil spirits to dwell in their hearts, what else are they doing but casting out demons? And what are believers doing, who give up the secular words of their former life and speak of the sacred mysteries and describe as far as they can the praise and power of their Creator, but speaking in new tongues? When they remove malice from the hearts of others by their good words of exhortation, they are picking up snakes, and when they hear dangerous advice, but are not drawn toward wicked deeds, they are indeed drinking something deadly, but that will not harm them." Is Olivi quoting Gregory directly or through Bede? See CCSL cxx, 646.

APPENDIX

ALBERT THE GREAT'S INTERPRETATION
OF PASSAGES WHICH ARE UNIQUE
TO MARK'S GOSPEL

INTRODUCTION

In the body of the annotated commentary I provided a few samples of the commentary by Albert the Great (d. 1280) on passages which are unique to Mark's Gospel. In this Appendix I provide more complete translations of Albert the Great's exposition of Mark 4:26-29, Mark 7:31-37, and Mark 8:22-26. I also give translations of selected passages from his commentary on Mark 9:30-10:52. Through these translations I want to supply my readers with the exegesis of a contemporary of Peter of John Olivi so that they can compare and contrast the work of these two commentators and thus arrive at some sense of what may be traditional and singular in Olivi's commentary.

MARK 4:26-29[1]

26) "And he said: Thus it is with the kingdom of God, as though a man should cast seed into the earth,"

27) "then sleep and rise, night and day, and the seed should sprout and grow without his knowing it."

28) "For of itself the earth bears the crop, first the blade, then the ear, then the full grain in the ear."

29) "But when the fruit is ripe, immediately he puts in the sickle because the harvest has come."

---

[1] See *In Marcum*, 434-36. My English translation of the Vulgate is based on *The Holy Bible: The Douay Version of The Old Testament; The Confraternity Edition of The New Testament*. (New York: P. J. Kenedy & Sons, 1950).

This deals with the increase in perfection of the ministers working in divine matters. It has two points: the way of the growth; the beginning and end of the growth. The beginning and consummation of the growth are touched upon in verse 30: "And he said: To what shall we liken?"[2]

Relative to the first point there are six concerns. The first deals with the comparison. The second treats the imperceptible growth. The third concentrates on its power. The fourth treats the stages of growth. The consummation of the growth forms the fifth point. The sixth concern is the opportune time when maturation is expected. All these issues are clear in a literal interpretation.

The text states: "And he said." Again he teaches the uneducated through the similitude of the parables. "Thus is the kingdom of God." He compares the kingdom of God to earthly matters. Job 38:33 says: "Do you know the order of heaven and can you provide the reason why the earth is?" "As though a man." A human situation is chosen since in human matters one obtains a clearer understanding because humans use reason. "A man should sow seed" in a cultivated field as has been already mentioned. Now the seed is the word of God. Jeremiah 4:3 states: "Break up anew your fallow ground and do not sow among thorns." "Upon the ground," which has been well cultivated since as the Philosopher says, "The farmer prepares the soil by plowing and planting."[3]

"And sleep," resting from this labor and thereby committing the harvest to the future. 1 Corinthians 3:7 reads: "Neither is the person who plants anything nor the person who waters, but it is God who gives the growth." "Sleeping" refers to the holy farmers since sleep indicates that death is at hand or perhaps it indicates contemplation and prayer in which they rest with God. Psalm 126:2-3 states: "When the Lord gives sleep to his beloved. Behold, the inheritance of the Lord are children, the reward, the fruit of the womb."

---

[2] I do not translate this second point. It deals with Mark 4:29, is short, and not interpreted by Olivi. See *In Marcum*, 436.

[3] See *In Marcum*, 435 where the critical edition gives no source for this "citation" from Aristotle.

"And rise," that is, the seed was continually increasing "night and day," always becoming better and stronger. 2 Samuel 3:1 says: "David was prospering and always growing stronger."

"And" with power fitting for its size, "the seed sprouts" up. Isaiah 66:14 says: "Your bones shall sprout like a herb," that is, with stronger powers. Psalm 91:13-14 states: "The just will sprout like the palm tree ... and will flourish forever before the Lord."

"And grow." Its increase led to the growth of its neighbors. Genesis 9:1 says: "Increase and multiply and fill the earth."

"Without his knowing it," that is, the sower, since in this life the preacher might not find out how the seed has grown into ripe fruit. And so it is said not only with regard to God in himself, but also with regard to God's own in Isaiah 45:15: "Truly you are a hidden God."

He gives the reason and the cause for this when he says: "For on its own." Not by the working of its essence, but through heavenly power, "the earth," which received a heavenly blessing, "bears the crop" by divine power. Genesis 27:28 reads: "May God give you moisture from heaven and from the abundance of the earth a fullness of grain and wine." And the text does not speak of your labor, because the moisture of heaven comes from God's grace and the abundance of the earth from the consolation of the Holy Spirit. They make the earth bring forth grain in the solid food of virtue and wine in spiritual joys and oil in the pouring forth of piety. This happens solely because of divine power.

Now it comes to fruition in stages. "First is the blade," a vigorous faith. Jeremiah 17:8 says: "He will be like a tree that is planted by the waters, that spreads out its roots toward moisture." But the Glossa states that the blade is found in fear which makes a person walk away from evil since, as it is said in Psalm 110:10, "the beginning of wisdom is fear of the Lord."

After the blade "then the ear," where the fruit is. Thus after a robust faith it produces shoots of virtues or after fear it produces penitence. Genesis 41:5 has: "Seven ears of grain on one stalk that was full and appealing." These are the seven virtues: the three theological virtues of faith, hope, and charity and the four cardinal virtues of prudence, justice, fortitude, and temperance. Or these are the seven parts of penitence: compunction of heart, oral confession, and satisfaction accomplished through works, namely, of prayer, fasting, and almsgiving. The seventh part, which is the very foundation of penitence, is the firm purpose of not sinning again. Thus, it produces the ear after a robust faith or fear.

"Then the full grain" comes in meritorious work that is done by charity. James 5:7 states: "Behold the farmer waits for the precious fruit of the earth, being patient until it receives the early and the late rain." And it bears fruit "in the ear," that is, in virtue or penitence.

"And when the fruit is ripe" and satisfactory. This deals with the time when the farmer who sowed the seed harvests it. Thus, "immediately he puts in," that is, he gathers this fruit for God in the heavenly barns. John 4:36 says: "The person who reaps receives a wage and gathers fruit unto life everlasting." Now by his diligence the preacher and prelate must gather such fruits for God and not seek personal gain from them. Matthew 13:30 has: "Gather the wheat into my barn." Luke 3:17 says: "He will gather the wheat into his barn, but the chaff he will burn up with unquenchable fire."

So he puts in "the sickle," since he removes the fruit from human praise and greed and puts it aside in God's barn, for this is the way that the Son assigned growth to his Holy Father as 1 Corinthians 15:24 states: "When he delivers the kingdom to God the Father."

"Because" at the time of the mature fruit "the harvest comes," so that all may be attributed to and reserved for God. And this happens either at the end of the world or at the end which death brings to each human being. Revelation 14:15 states: "Put forth your sickle and reap since the hour to reap has come, because the harvest of the earth is ripe."

MARK 7:31-37[4]

31) "And departing again from the district of Tyre, he came by way of Sidon to the Sea of Galilee, through the midst of the district of the Decapolis." This passage shows how the power of the Lion from the tribe of Judah cures actual sin. This cure is against the actual sin that is manifested and performed in the members of the body, armed by the iniquity of sin. This section has two parts. The first deals with the place where the miracle is performed. The second narrates the performance of the miracle.

Relative to the first point, the text says this about the place he had just left: "And departing again from the district of Tyre," where Jews and Gentiles lived together. He left there so that he might communicate and preach his grace to the indigent in other places. Luke 4:43 says: "I must also proclaim the good news of the kingdom of God to other towns because this is why I have been sent."

"He came by way of Sidon," passing through as a hunter of souls, for Sidon means hunting. Genesis 27:3-4 states: "When you have taken something by hunting, make me a savory meal from it as you know I like and bring it for me to eat." This is what the Patriarch said to his son. He was passing through "to the Sea of Galilee," that is, Lake Gennesaret. This Galilee, in as far as it is part of the province in which he was traveling, "is through the midst of the district of the Decapolis." Decapolis refers to the ten cities to be built there, whose territories bordered one another there. The Decapolis signifies congregations of the faithful who are bound by the ten commandments of the Decalogue. Luke 19:17 says: "You will have power over ten cities."

32) "And they brought him a man who was deaf and dumb and implored him to lay his hand upon him." The second point is the story of the miracle which has three components: the pleading for a miracle; the special way of performing the miracle; the miracle's usefulness for edification.

---

[4] See *In Marcum*, 504-07.

There are three parts to the pleading: bringing the person forward; the intercession; the imposition of a hand. Relative to bringing the person forward the text says: "And they brought to him," because of their zealous faith. Psalm 28:1 states: "Bring to the Lord, you children of God, bring to the Lord the offspring of rams," that is, the offspring of prelates and preachers. Now these rams are the leaders of the flock, and they must lead to the Lord the offspring committed to them so that they may be cured.

He is "deaf," because the arms of iniquity had attacked his ears by sin. Thus the devil had brought about deafness in the ears, especially a deafness to hear the word of God. This is because the first mother had opened her ears in this way to the serpent. So too had the first father opened his ears to the woman who had been persuaded by the serpent.

He was also "dumb," for every deaf person is naturally mute, since he cannot learn what to say through hearing it. Furthermore, this individual also had a tongue that was tied so that he could not move it to speak. Thus it is said in verse 35 below: "the bond of his tongue was loosed." Ezekiel 3:26 reads: "I will make your tongue stick fast to the roof of your mouth, and you will be dumb." Psalm 37:14 says: "I, as a deaf man, did not hear, and as a dumb man who does not open his mouth." And this also was fittingly incurred because of the first transgression, in which the tongue had been loosed to speak with the serpent against God. Psalm 136:6 states: "Let my tongue cleave to my jaws if I do not remember you," that is, I will not remember you, but rather the words of the devil with whom you are speaking.

"And they implored him," that is, the Lord. And this is the intercession made by those standing about. This signifies the intercession of Holy Church. James 5:16 says: "Pray for one another that you may be saved, for the unceasing prayer of a just person avails much."

"That he impose upon him," the deaf and mute man, "his hand," a hand which is all powerful and which created him and has the power also to reform what was corrupt. Job 5:18 has: "He wounds and cures. He strikes, and his hands will heal." Psalm 138:5-6 states: "You have laid your hand over me. Your knowledge has become wonderful to me. It is exalted, and I cannot reach it." Those interceding knew what is said in Job 26:13: "By his obstetric hand the winding serpent was brought forth."[5] And so they had asked that he grant this benefit by using his hand. Mark 16:18 reads: "They will lay hands upon the sick, and they will get well."

33) "And taking him aside from the crowd, he put his fingers into the man's ears, and spitting, he touched his tongue." This verse focuses in a double way on the way the miracle was performed. First is what the Lord did. The second focus is on the sick man.

With regard to the Lord there are three points: deeds, perspectives, and words. There are four types of deeds. First is the manner of taking a person aside.[6] In this instance the Lord binds himself with the sick man, and this signifies embracing a person with compassion and love. With these God embraces us. Hebrews 2:16 states: "He is not embracing the angels, but the offspring of Abraham." And this is the meaning of "taking him aside." Philippians 3:12 states: "I follow, hoping that I may lay hold of that for which Christ Jesus has laid hold of me."

Second the person whom Christ had taken aside is separated from the crowd. This signifies separation from the mass of perdition and from those who have perished. This is accomplished through the taking hold of grace. Numbers 16:26 says: "Depart from the tents of these wicked people and touch nothing of theirs, lest you be involved in their sins." Galatians 1:15-16 has: "When it pleased him who from my mother's womb set me apart and called me by his grace to

---

[5] It seems that Albert the Great has selected Job 26:13 as an interpretive passage because it contains the words "hand" and "serpent." However, its meaning is relatively obscure. The NAB translates the Hebrew: "His hand pierces the fugitive dragon as from his hand it strives to flee."

[6] Albert the Great plays on the various meanings of the Latin verb *apprehendere*. See Leo F. Stelten, *Dictionary of Ecclesiastical Latin*. (Peabody, MA: Hendrickson, 1995), 20: "take hold of, seize, apprehend, press to, embrace, lay hands on."

reveal his Son in me that I might preach him among the Gentiles, I did not immediately consult with flesh and blood." There is separation from the womb of Mother Synagogue. There is separation from the mass of perdition. This is what is meant when the text says: "aside from the crowd."

The third action is that "he put his fingers into his ears." These fingers signify the creative power by which he created all things through power, wisdom, and goodness. Isaiah 40:12 states: "Who has held the bulk of the earth with three fingers?" These are the first three fingers. Now the finger points to the power of the Holy Spirit through the gifts of wisdom and understanding, etc., which Isaiah enumerates.[7] Luke 11:20 says: "If I cast out demons by the finger of God, then the kingdom of God has come upon you." It is also precisely through his fingers that he performs the work of redemption in the great bitterness of the passion. *The Song of Songs* 5:5 states: "My hands dripped with myrrh, and my fingers were full of the choicest myrrh." No power of the demon enemy could stand against these fingers because the first fingers cast out the inability to hear and the non-perception of what must be heard. They also cast out malice against the divine things that have been heard. The fourth finger casts out sin through the gift of the Holy Spirit. Through the fifth finger he removes the bondage of being deaf by paying the price of its liberation through the passion. He inserts these intellectual fingers which are internal and spiritual rather than his bodily fingers in an external fashion. Thereby, he has touched the man interiorly with them and has cast out demonic power. The text says: "into his ears," since he has ears that only have the appearance of ears, but do not have the power of hearing. His hearing is diminished and imperfect.

"And spitting, he touched his tongue." This is the fourth action. Spittle that descends from the head signifies the taste for divine things. This taste travels to the tongue and loosens

---

[7] See Isa 11:2-3: "And the spirit of the Lord will rest upon him, the spirit of wisdom and understanding, the spirit of counsel and fortitude, the spirit of knowledge and of godliness. And the spirit of the fear of the Lord will fill him."

the bond that impedes speaking. 1 Samuel 14:29 states: "You yourselves have seen that my eyes have been enlightened, because I have tasted a little of this honey." Now I see what is to be tasted and spoken. Further the honey that is under the tongue of the Lord signifies the sweetness of his teaching. The Song of Songs 4:11 has: "Honey and milk are under your tongue." So by this honey he touches his tongue.

34) "And looking up to heaven, he sighed and said to him: Ephphetha, that is, be opened." Here two ways of looking are mentioned. The first takes place with the eyes of the body and signifies that he refers all things to the Father in the harmony and unity he has towards him. The other is of the heart which is signified by his sigh, by which he sighs on our behalf. This is what is meant by "he sighed." John 11:41 refers to the first seeing: "Jesus, raising his eyes, said: Father, I give you thanks that you have heard me." Thus he teaches us to direct our intentions heavenward when we want to ask for anything. 2 Chronicles 20:12 says: "Since we don't know what to do, we can only turn our eyes to you." *The Song of Songs* 2:12 speaks of this sighing: "The voice of the turtledove is heard in our land." The turtledove's song is a sigh. Psalm 37:9 states: "I called aloud with the sighing of my heart."

"And he said: Ephphetha," in Hebrew. This deals with the verbal component of the miracle. The Evangelist interprets this command: "That is, be opened," referring to opening the bonds of the ears and of the tongue, so that he might hear and speak. Isaiah 50:5 says: "The Lord God has opened my ear, and I do not resist and do not go back." Isaiah 50:4 states: "The Lord has given me a learned tongue, so that I may know how to sustain the weary by my word."

35) "And immediately his ears were opened, and the bond of his tongue was loosed, and he began to speak correctly." This verse treats the effect the miracle has on the sick person. There are three points. The first concerns the ears. "And immediately his ears were opened." Earlier they had only the external appearance of ears, but now they are made to be

truly ears and hear. "They were opened," so that sound and voices may enter and be heard. Proverbs 20:12 says: "The ear that hears and the eye that sees, the Lord has made them both." Isaiah 35:5 states: "Then will the eyes of the blind be opened, and the ears of the deaf be unstopped."

"And the bond of his tongue was loosed." This is the second point and concerns the tongue. Isaiah 35:6 reads: "And the tongue of the dumb will be opened." Luke 11:14 has: "Jesus was casting out a demon, and it was dumb. And when he had cast out the demon, the dumb man spoke."

"And he began to speak correctly." The third point concentrates on the act that demonstrates that the bonds of his tongue and ears had been loosed, for he would not have spoken unless he had heard. Isaiah 32:3-4 says: "The eyes of those who see will not be dim, and the ears of those who hear will listen attentively. And the heart of fools will understand knowledge, and the tongue of stammerers will speak readily and plainly."

36) "And he charged them to tell no one." This verse touches on the edification that followed upon the miracle. Two points are made: the edification provided by the Lord's humility; the edification stemming from the divine praise uttered by the crowd and friends of the man cured. The text says: "And he charged them." This is not a precept to be observed. Rather it is one of instruction, namely, when great deeds have been done, be humble and follow the Lord's example. "To tell no one," so that through this command they might learn not to boast of the good they do. Sirach 3:20 states: "The greater you are, the more you should humble yourself in all things." Matthew 11:29 reads: "Learn from me, for I am meek and humble of heart."

37) "But the more he charged them, the more did they continue to broadcast it. And so much the more did they wonder, saying: He has done all things well. He has made the deaf to hear and the dumb to speak."[8]

---

[8] Albert the Great combines what we would call Mark 4:36b and 4:37.

Here is the second type of edification, and three points are made: edification for greater glory; edification for greater wonder; edification for greater praise. "The more he charged them," and with greatest humility and by means of a precept of instruction, "the more did they continue to broadcast" his glory. The reason is, as Cicero states at the end of the first book of his *Rhetoric*, "glory is public praise voiced by many." Tobit 12:7 says: "It is honorable to reveal ... the works of God." Isaiah 66:19 reads: "And they will declare my glory to the Gentiles."

"And so much more did they wonder," because he, out of humility, commanded that this miracle should not be broadcast about. Esther 15:17 has: "Lord, you are completely full of wonders, and your face is replete with graces." What is especially wonderful is that on such a face, resplendent with grace, there was such humility. "Saying," in the sublime edification of praise, "he has done all things well," that is, he proved that he himself could do all things well. That is, he demonstrated his omnipotence. Romans 9:19 says: "Who resists his will?"

"He has made the deaf to hear," as many as he wished, and the dumb to speak, for first the deaf must hear so that they know what to say. Proverbs 18:13 states: "The person who responds before he hears something demonstrates that he is a fool and worthy of shame."

So in this way the power of the Lion heals actual sin.

MARK 8:22-26[9]

22) "And they came to Bethsaida, and they brought him a blind man and entreated him to touch him." This verse introduces a miracle whose purpose is to remove a defect left by sin, namely, darkness of the heart.

There are two parts. In the first the power of the Lion is manifested in the miracle. But since the power shown is still not sufficiently understood, the second part adds the teaching by which it is explained where verse 27 says: "And Jesus and his disciples went out into the villages."

---

[9] See *In Marcum*, 524-27.

The miracle story is divided into three parts. The first foregrounds the devotion of the people who are asking for the miracle. The second describes the miracle. In the third there is teaching about humility to counter the exaltation which customarily arises from great deeds.

In the first part there are three components, namely, the appropriateness of the place; the dignity of the people who brought the blind man to Jesus; the simplicity of their petition.

The text states: "And they came to Bethsaida," which is a city beyond the Sea of Galilee. It was the hometown of Andrew and Peter and Philip and Nathanael, his brother. And thus to honor such a place it was fitting that a miracle occur there. Further, since Bethsaida means "house of hunting," it was fitting that the Son be blessed by God in his hunting so that he might offer a savory dish to God the Father Almighty. Jeremiah 16:16 says: "I will send them many hunters, and they will hunt them." Genesis 27:4 states: "Offer me [a savory dish] from your hunting that I may eat, and my soul may bless you."

"And they brought him," they are worthy to bring him because they were known to the Apostles, being fellow citizens. "The blind man," is fittingly led to the illuminator. John 9:5 states: "While I am in the world, I am the light of the world." Likewise John 9:39 reads: "For judgment I have come into this world that they who do not see may see." Their bringing the blind man forth indicates their devotion and faith. Through these they are worthy to obtain what they petition. Matthew 21:2 says: "Loose and bring to me."[10]

"And they entreated him." Look at the simplicity of their petition. James 5:16 has: "Pray for one another that you may be saved, for the unceasing prayer of a just person avails much." "To touch him," firmly believing that with the touch of his hand, deity being united to this hand, he might bring about salvation. Job 5:18 states: "He strikes, and his hands

---

[10] Matt 22:2 says: "[Jesus] saying to them: Go into the village opposite you, and immediately you will find an ass tied and a colt with her. Loose them and bring them to me."

shall heal." Now just as they sought an outward touch, so too were they petitioning for the inward touch of compunction, realizing that unless sin is removed interiorly, the outside infirmity is not cured. And this is what the Interlinear Gloss says: "The person is touched who has compunction." Psalm 143:5 reads: "Touch the mountains," that is, the proud, "and they will smoke."

23) "And taking the blind man by the hand, he led him forth outside the village. And applying spittle to his eyes, he laid his hands upon him and asked him whether he saw anything." This treats the performance of the miracle which is twofold. The first signifies the difficulty of purging the remnants of sin. The other signifies what the power of the physician accomplishes.

The first one has two components. One focuses on the physician who has power over sickness. The other underscores the difficulty of curing the infirm person.

Relative to the first significance of the miracle there are four considerations. The first is the coming together of the physician and the infirm person where the text says: "And taking the blind man by the hand," that is, the power through which the blind man acts, so that interiorly that power will not place an obstacle to the working of grace. So the hand of grace takes and holds on to the blind man's power to act. Psalm 72:24 says: "You have held me by my right hand, and by your will you have led me. And with your glory you have accepted me." For this is the hand that created and now takes hold lest he escape from re-creation as he escaped from creation. Job 10:8 states: "Your hands have made me and fashioned me wholly round about. And are you going to suddenly cast me down headlong?" Now if someone asks why he took the man by the hand when he needed to cure his eyes, we will say, as the Philosopher does, that the hand is understood as an instrument and organ. It is an instrument fit for diverse activities,[11] but these diverse activities are not fitting unless

---

[11] See Book IV, c. 10 of Aristotle, *De partibus animalium* in WAE, Volume 5, 687a: "... we must conclude that man does not owe his superior

they accord with the intellect which is the interior eye. And so in order to signify that the cause begins from the interior, he takes hold of the instrument that the intellect employs. Wherefore, the Glossa says that he takes hold of the hand, so that he might strengthen him for a good work. Matthew 8:3 says: "And stretching forth his hand, Jesus touched him."

"He led him forth outside the village." Second is the removal of the impediment to the cure, since in the tumult of the village where there is occasion of sin a person cannot be cured. In these villages and streets, that is, in the narrow and broad streets of concupiscence the spouse does not find God. Isaiah 43:8 says: "Bring forth the people that is blind." Genesis 19:17 states: "Do not stay in all the country about, but save yourself on the mountain," namely, away from humans who are sinners.

"And applying spittle on his eyes." Third is the application of a taste for divine wisdom because saliva both descends from the head and has the taste of salt. It also signifies the gift of wisdom that descends from the head of the Christ of God and that by its taste takes away the taste of sin which covered the interior eye with a veil. That is why John 9:11 states: "He made clay and anointed my eyes and said to me: Go to the pool of Siloam and wash. And I went and washed, and I see." Thus, the Glossa comments: "Applying spittle so that he might see the will of God through the breath of the Holy Spirit."

"He laid his hands upon him." The fourth point signifies an exterior example that demonstrates in his humanity that his light had the purpose of giving light. John 8:12 says: "I am the light of the world. The person who follows me does not walk in darkness." Wherefore, in Matthew 5:16 it was also said to the Apostles who were following the example of

---

intelligence to his hands, but his hands to his superior intelligence. For the most intelligent of animals is the one who would put the most organs to use; and the hand is not to be looked on as one organ but as many; for it is, as it were, an instrument for further instruments. This instrument, therefore, – the hand – of all instruments the most serviceable, has been given by nature to man, the animal of all animals the most capable of acquiring the most varied handicrafts."

the Lord: "Let your light shine before men and women so that they may see your good deeds and give glory to your Father who is in heaven."

These are the four things that have been utilized. Interiorly there is the help of grace and the application of wisdom. Exteriorly there is the removal of the impediment and the offering of an example. The text continues: "He asked him whether he saw anything." He asked not because he did not know, but in order to teach that an interior defect (which stems from sin) is not healed without our will and consent since Wisdom 1:4 states: "Wisdom will not enter into a malicious soul nor dwell in a body subject to sins," that is, that wants to continue to be subject to sins. So he was asking so that he might elicit consent for the cure, not that he might learn something he did not know.

24) "And he looked up and said: I see human beings as though they were trees walking about." This verse sets forth the beginning of the cure from the perspective of the sick person and signifies the difficulty of removing the remainder (or the remnants) of sin. So the text states that "he looked up," that is, he was now beginning to see. "He said," signifying that some bit of the light of grace was apparent to him. Daniel 7:7 says: "I saw in a vision of the night," that is, by means of sight that is still obscured by darkness.

"I saw," by a vision of grace, rational "human beings," whom, before I was cured to see rational beings, I saw "as though they were trees," because he had blurred vision. And because of a humor he had vision that was not focused. For such people things that are near seem far away and small things seem gigantic.

"Walking," since for such infirm people even those things that are standing seem to be moving. This is clear to all from experience when people have impaired vision because of a humor moving into the pupil of the eye. On a spiritual level these things signify that as long as anyone has a virulent humor of concupiscence spreading over the eye of the heart, the intellect cannot have vision that is in focus. And this is the case since he has been in darkness due to a longstanding blindness. So left to his own, he cannot find light in a flash. Psalm 37:11 states: "My heart is troubled. My strength has left me, and my eyes have no light."

25) "Then again he imposed his hands upon his eyes, and he began to see and was restored so that he saw all things clearly." This verse highlights the power of the Lion from the tribe of Judah over the blindness brought about by the enemy of light: "Again he imposed his hands upon the man's eyes." This second imposition of hands signifies the power of liberating grace that came from Christ, for it removes all blindness from us. John 1:4-5 states: "In him was life, and the life was the light of human beings. And the light shone in the darkness, and the darkness did not comprehend it." Rather the light itself has dissipated all darkness. This is what the text says: "And he began to see" clearly "and was restored" to health, "so that he saw clearly," that is, distinctly and individually, "all things" that are visible. Psalm 12:4 reads: "Enlighten my eyes that I may never sleep in death," since in sleep the eyes are darkened. Psalm 118:18 says: "Open my eyes, and I will consider the wondrous things of your law."

26) "And he sent him to his house, saying: Go to your house, and if you enter the village, tell no one." This verse gives two warnings to the person who had been healed, that is, how he should take care of himself and about humble conduct.

There are two points to how he should care for himself and are found in the words: "And he sent him to his house," so that he might scrutinize the family of his own house lest there be any occasion of sin in it. Proverbs 31:27 states: "She scrutinized the ways of her house and did not eat her food in idleness." Genesis 18:19 says: "I know that he will command his children and the members of his house," namely, that they fear me.

"Saying: Go to your house." This treats of how you should care for yourself. Wisdom 8:16 has: "When I enter my house,

I will repose with wisdom, for conversation with her has no bitterness. Companionship with her is not boring."

"And if you enter the village." This is a precept about how he should take care of himself. To enter a village is to rub shoulders with the clean and with sinners, to walk in the midst of a depraved and perverse people. The holy man enters such a village to convert the people. 2 Peter 2:8 states: "Their wicked deeds which the just man saw and heard while living among them tormented his just soul day after day."

"Tell nobody," to prevent pride and vanity. However, he could and should say something to proclaim God's praises. Psalm 38:2 and 10 say: "I have set a guard on my mouth when the sinner stood against me.... I was dumb and did not open my mouth."

In conclusion, this is the teaching about the meaning of this miracle story: it is against the defect introduced by sin.

SELECTED PASSAGES FROM MARK 9:30-10:52[12]

MARK 9:37-39[13]

37) "John said to him: Master, we saw a man who was not one of our followers, casting out demons in your name, and we forbade him."

38) "But Jesus said: "Do not forbid him, because there is no one who works a miracle in my name and then immediately speaks evil of me."

39) "For the person who is not against you is for you."

This passage implicitly sets forth the situation of a person coming and teaching the sound doctrine of the little ones. Although that person does not live the life of the apostles, he should not be treated as an outcast, but accepted and paid for his ministry. This is how this passage is to be interpreted. And so two things are being highlighted here, namely, the perverse perspective of the Apostles that would ban such

---

[12] See *In Marcum*, 559-618.
[13] See *In Marcum*, 564-65.

people; the correction of this perversity so that the right understanding of the truth of the Gospel might shine forth.

The text says: "Master," for it is his teaching that is on trial. "We saw," here John is speaking on behalf of all the Apostles. "A man," who is not worthy to be given a name. Psalm 15:4: "I will not remember their names and speak them."

"In your name," that is, who has faith in your name. And this could not take place unless the person possessed sound teaching. "Casting out demons," by the finger of God, that is, he was casting out the demons in a demonstration of divine power. Luke 11:20 states: "If I cast out demons by the finger of God, then the kingdom of God has come upon you."

"Who does not follow," you whom we follow, by reason of virtue and imitation of holiness. He is not with us, and "we forbade him." We wished that whoever proclaims you is fit apostolically, both by reason of virtue and from the sound teaching of the truth in word. But this would generate great harm in the Church since many proclaim Christ in the Church, not by reason of their [apostolic] life, but rather because of their good deeds. Thus Philippians 1:17 states: "Some proclaim Christ out of contentiousness and not sincerely ..." A little later verse 18 says: "But what of it? Provided only that in every way, whether in pretense or in truth, Christ is being proclaimed. In this I rejoice. Yes, and I will rejoice." And so Christ corrects this error in the Apostles.

This occurs where the text states: "But Jesus said." He was teaching them to tolerate such people. "Do not forbid him," since although he may be harming himself, he is benefiting many in the Church. Matthew 23:3 states: "Do what they say, but do not act according to their deeds." For in their praising God they speak the language of the angels, and in their teaching of the faith they speak human language. But if they do not have charity, they may benefit others by the words they speak while at the same time hurt themselves. 1 Corinthians 13:1 says: "If I should speak with angelic and human tongues, but do not have charity, I have become as a sounding brass or a tinkling cymbal."

"Because there is no one who works a miracle," or sign "in my name," making note of me in his teaching, "and can" fittingly and "immediately speak evil of me," since unless he subverts his teaching about me, he cannot speak evil of me. And this he cannot immediately do as long as he is invoking the name of Christ. Matthew 7:22-23 reads: "Lord, Lord, did we not perform many miracles in your name? And then he will declare to them: I never knew you."

"For the person who is not against you," by perverse teaching is "for you," because he is teaching the same thing as you are. And therefore, as the Glossa says, he is not to be prevented from what he has, but rather to be prompted to acquire what he does not have. Luke 9:50 says: "Do not forbid him, for the person who is not against you is for you." However, if he is an enemy to sound teaching and is teaching perverse things, he should be forbidden, for about such a person Matthew 12:30 and Luke 11:23 say: "The person who is not with me is against me, and the person who does not gather with me scatters."

MARK 10:21B-22[14]

21b-22) "And he said to him: You lack one thing. Go, sell whatever you have, and give to the poor, and you will have treasure in heaven. And come, follow me. But he was saddened by the saying and went away sorrowful, for he had great possessions."

He adds the height of perfection attained through the observance of the counsels. There are two points. In the first he shows that in the observance of the commandments there is something lacking in perfection. In the second he shows the more sublime way of perfection. So he says: "You lack one thing." The Glossa comments: for perfection. Philippians 3:12 states: "Not that I have already obtained this or already have been made perfect." Psalm 138:16 says: "Your eyes have seen my imperfect being." Daniel 5:27 has: "You are weighed in the balance and are found wanting."

---

[14] See *In Marcum*, 598-99.

"Go," etc. He mentions six things that are pertinent to perfection. The first is progress in virtue. Second is the complete stripping of worldly wealth. Third is the goodness of almsgiving. Fourth is a single-minded focus and intention. Fifth is devoted imitation. Sixth is the perfect following of Christ, and this is primary in this work.

So the text says: "Go," not by steps made by one's feet, but rather by steps made along the way of virtue. Psalm 83:8 says: "They will go from virtue to virtue. The God of gods will be seen in Zion." Ezekiel 1:14 has: "The living creatures ran ... like flashes of lightning."

"Sell whatever you have," if you have these things in your power. Jerome comments: "If you have your possessions in your power, sell them. If you do not, throw them away. The entire world of riches belongs to the believer while the non-believer doesn't even have a penny." Luke 12:33 has: "Sell what you possess and give alms." Luke 16:9 states: "Make friends for yourselves of the mammon of iniquity, so that when you fail they may receive you into the everlasting dwellings."

"And give to the poor." Here is the goodness of almsgiving. One should give to the poor who have no riches and no means to return the favor. Tobit 4:9 says: "If you have much, give generously. If you have little, take care to freely give from what little you have." Isaiah 58:7 states: "Share your food with the hungry. Bring the needy and the homeless into your home." Psalm 111:9 has: "He has made distribution and given to the poor. His justice remains forever and ever."

"And you will have treasure in heaven." Here is the single-minded focus and intention. Matthew 6:20 reads: "Lay up for yourselves treasures in heaven where neither rust nor moth consumes nor thieves break in and steal." Now these treasures are the accumulation of holy merits and rewards. 2 Timothy 1:12 says: "I know whom I have believed and am certain that he is able to guard the trust committed to me against that day."

"And come," through imitation. Jeremiah 51:50 states: "Come away. Don't stand still. Remember the Lord from far off, and let Jerusalem come into your heart." Matthew 11:28

says: "Come to me, all you who labor and are heavily burdened, and I will give you rest."

"Follow me," through perfect following. Matthew 4:19 has: "Come after me. The Glossa comments: "Walk as I walk." 1 John 2:6 reads: "The person who says that he abides in Christ must for his part walk as he has walked."

"He was saddened by the saying." The text continues: "He went away sorrowful." This is a sign of imperfection in not observing the counsels. The text says well that "he went away," because although he had tasted divine reality and love, he regressed to what was familiar. Ezekiel 3:14 states: "I went away in bitterness, and my spirit was indignant." The text adds the reason for his sorrow when it says "for he possessed," and was possessed by them, "many possessions." He truly wanted these possessions to remain with him and to give him total peace.[15] Matthew 19:22 says: "When the young man heard the saying, he went away sad, for he had great possessions." Jerome in the Glossa comments: "Possessions are like thorns and briars that spring up and choke the seed sown by the Lord."

MARK 10:46-52[16]

46) "And they came to Jericho. And as he was leaving with his disciples and a very large crowd, Bartimaeus, a blind man, the son of Timaeus, was sitting by the wayside, begging."

Here Mark takes on the face of the Lion and shows that a miracle confirms the aforementioned teaching.[17] There are four components to this story. The first one accentuates the antecedents to the plea for the miracle. The second one focuses on the person to be cured. The third one underlines the

---

[15] See *In Marcum*, 598 for Albert the Great's earlier comment: "But he was sad about giving away all his possessions and about begging. And this is not contrary to salvation, but to perfection according to the state of the greatest poverty."

[16] See *In Marcum*, 614-18.

[17] Does this teaching go back to Mark 8:31 and include the three predictions of the passion?

circumstances around the Savior's miracle. The fourth and final one deals with the consequences of the miracle.

The first component has four considerations: place, journey, the edification of the disciples, and the great crowd that was accompanying him. About the first the text says: "And they came," as they journeyed towards Jerusalem, "to Jericho." Mark omits what Matthew 20 had also omitted, namely, what is contained in Luke 18:35-19:10. So after narrating that on coming into Jericho the Savior gave sight to a blind man, Luke tells the story that as Christ was leaving Jericho, he addressed Zacchaeus and accepted hospitality from him. On account of the merit of his hospitality he was justified as his name fittingly means. This all fits together because Jericho means "moon," for the moon is an entity that continuously borrows its light from the sun. In the same way Zacchaeus is justified and the blind man is given light by the borrowed light coming from the Sun of justice. Sirach 43:7 states: "From the moon comes the sign of a festival day. It is a light that decreases in its course." Psalm 88:38 says: "And the moon is a faithful witness in the heavens."

"And as he was leaving," that is, Christ "from Jericho." Jesus is on his journey to Jerusalem, hastening to his passion. He is also giving us an example. Hebrews 12:2 says: "Look towards the author and finisher of faith, Jesus, who for the joy set before him, endured a cross and despised shame." "His disciples" were with him. They were to be instructed and strengthened by the miracle. John 2:11 reads: "Jesus performed the first of his signs before his disciples, and he manifested his glory and his disciples believed in him."

With him was "a great crowd," which was piously going up to Jerusalem with the Lord for the festive day. The miracle would build up their faith. Revelation 7:9 has: "I saw a great crowd which no one could number, out of all nations ... standing before the throne." Isaiah 2:3 says: "And many people will go and say: Come, let us ascend to the mountain of the Lord and to the house of the God of Jacob. And he will teach us his ways, and we will walk in his paths."

"Son of Timaeus." The text deals now with the person who experiences the miracle. There are three considerations: the happiness of an earlier prosperity; the unhappiness of sudden misery; his constant supplication that calls attention to himself. Note that Matthew 20:30-34 mentions the Lord gave sight to two blind men. Mark, however, singles out the more notable one. He does not deny that there was another blind man, but remains silent about him. Thus Bede in the Glossa remarks: "Matthew indicates that two blind men sitting by the wayside were given sight. Luke follows the same sequence of events and writes that as Christ was approaching Jericho, he gave sight to one blind man. Luke, for his part, mentions what Matthew omits. Now while Matthew mentions two blind men, Mark says that there was one. He is not denying the existence of the second blind man. Rather he wants to point out that the one he mentions was more famous. That is why Mark notes the man's name and that of his father. He does not do this in other instances except when he names Jairus. The reason behind Mark's action is that this man was noble and has now been cast down into unhappiness since he is not only blind, but must sit along the wayside begging." Mark describes the cure of this blind man and contrasts his former high status with Christ's miracle. This is why the text says: "Son of Timaeus," a noble man, whose name is "Bartimaeus," which means "son of abundance." This name indicates his former prosperity. Job 16:13 states: "I was formerly wealthy, and then I was broken into pieces." Luke 1:52 reads: "He has cast down the mighty from their thrones."

"A blind man." From such a high level of prosperity this man has fallen into a twofold miserable condition. He is "blind," so that he cannot see the road he must travel to obtain the necessities of life. Moreover "he was sitting," since he had no one to guide him on the road. Lamentations 3:2 reads: "He has led me, bringing me into darkness and not into the light."

He was "by the wayside," not on the road so that he wouldn't become an obstacle to those passing by and so that he could be seen by those passing by. Matthew 20:30 says: "Two blind men were sitting by the road." Isaiah 59:9 states: "We looked for light, and behold there was darkness; for brightness, and we walked in darkness." Perhaps he had fallen into the miseries of blindness and became a poor beggar because he had misused his prosperity. Deuteronomy 28:29 reads: "May you grope at bright midday as the blind person is wont to grope in the dark, and may you not find the right way."

"Begging," that is, by extending his hand he was declaring his poverty, and in his miserable bodily condition he had no consolation in life and no way out of his misery. Job 30:3 states: "Sterile with want and hunger ... disfigured with calamity and misery." Qoheleth 5:12-13 says: "There is another ... evil which I have seen under the sun: riches preserved to the hurt of their owner, for they are lost with very great affliction. He has begotten a son who will be in extremity of want."

47) "And hearing that it was Jesus of Nazareth, he began to cry out and say: Jesus, Son of David, have mercy on me." Here we encounter the insistent supplicant. There are two points: the supplication and the insistence. Relative to the supplication there are three considerations: his rising to make his petition; his intense crying out; the title he invokes in making his supplication.

The text states: "And hearing," from the passersby since as Luke 18:36-37 reads: "When he heard a crowd passing by, he asked what was going on. They told him that Jesus of Nazareth was passing by."

"That it was Jesus of Nazareth," blossoming with every flower, passing by, he hoped for mercy and goodness and largess from him who was enlightening every person coming into this world. He was spurred to ask him, about whom Luke 1:79 said: "to shine on those who sit in darkness and in the shadow of death, to guide our feet into the way of peace." "He began to cry out" with a very strong voice. His desire and purpose were great. Psalm 17:7 has: "My clamor burst upon his ears." Psalm 118:145 says: "I cried with all my heart:

Hear me, O Lord." Baruch 3:1 has: "The soul in anguish and the troubled spirit cry out to you, O Lord."

"And said." The blind man selects the title he will use in his petition. "Jesus, son of David, have mercy on me." He calls Jesus, Savior, whose office and deeds always deal with salvation. Towards the end of the Prayer of Manasseh the text reads: "You will save unworthy me in accordance with your great mercy."

"Son of David," who have a mighty hand and can save with loving affection. Because of your graciousness you extend to all your grace-filled countenance. You have kingly riches by which you can save. You even have mercy on your enemies whose hearts you afflict with pangs of conscience and compel them to have mercy. You are his son, and as an inheritance have accepted all things. You, "have mercy on me." With regard to the first Sirach 46:1-2 says: "Jesus, son of Nun ... who was great according to his name, and was very great for the salvation of God's elect." With regard to the second Joel 2:13 states: "God is gracious and merciful ... willing to relent in punishing." Esther 15:17 has: "O Lord, you are worthy of all admiration, and your face is full of graces." With regard to the third 1 Corinthians 1:5 says: "In everything you have been enriched in him." And verse 7 continues: "so that you lack no grace." Romans 10:12 states: "He is rich towards all who call upon him." About the fourth, Psalm 129:7 reads: "With the Lord is mercy, and with him is plenteous redemption."

Wherefore, "have mercy on me." Through your compassion remove the miseries that afflict my body and indicate my bad luck. Psalm 50:3 says: "Have mercy on me, O God, according to your great mercy." Isaiah 63:15 states: "Where are your zeal and your strength, the multitude of your mercies and your compassion? They have hidden themselves from me."

48) "And many angrily tried to silence him. But he cried out all the louder: Son of David, have mercy on me." This verse accentuates insistent petitioning. Three matters clamor for attention: the menace of those rebuking who were unable to get him to shut up; the continuous nature of his loud

cries; the repetition of his supplication. Thus, the text says: "And many angrily tried," not wishing to disturb the Lord, "to silence him." Luke 18:39 states: "Those who went in front angrily tried to silence him, but he cried out all the louder." Such people signify those who would drag a person away from a good work. Proverbs 3:27 has: "Do not prohibit a person from doing the good work he is capable of doing. If you are able, you yourself do good."

"But he cried out all the louder." Colossians 4:2 reads: "Be steadfast in prayer; be vigilant in prayer." Luke 18:1 says: "They must always pray and not lose heart." Lamentations 2:18 states: "Let tears run down like a torrent day and night. Give yourself no rest, and let not the apple of your eye keep quiet."

"Son of David, have mercy on me." He repeats his petition. Matthew 15:22 has: "Have mercy on me, Lord, Son of David," for David was prompt and eager to please, and you are his heir. 2 Samuel 23:8 states: "He was like the most tender worm of the wood."[18] Habakkuk 1:2 says: "How long, O Lord, will I cry and you will not hear? Shall I cry out to you as I suffer violence, and you will not save me?"

49) "Then Jesus stopped and ordered that he should be summoned. And they summoned the blind man and said to him: Take courage. Get up. He is calling you."

50) "And throwing off his cloak, he sprang to his feet and came to him."

51) "And Jesus addressed him and said: What do you want me to do for you? The blind man said to him: Rabboni, that I may see."

---

[18] 2 Samuel 23:8 talks about one of David's best men who killed 800 in one battle. The Latin behind "the most tender worm of the wood" is not found in the Hebrew. In the NAB 2 Sam 23:8 states: "These are the names of David's warriors. Ishbaal, son of Hachamoni, was the first of the Three. It was he who brandished his battle-ax over eight hundred slain in a single encounter."

52) "And Jesus said to him: Go on your way. Your faith has saved you. And immediately he began to see and followed him along the way."

These verses detail the circumstances surrounding this miracle. There are seven. First is the position of the healer: "Then Jesus stopped," so that the blind man could come to him. He stopped out of mercy and waited for him, whom in justice he would free from his condition of begging. Isaiah 30:18 states: "The Lord waits that he may have mercy on you." *The Song of Songs* 2:9 says: "Behold he stands behind our wall." And what is wonderful is that he is standing and waiting while earlier the blind man had stood and knocked.

Second is the command to bring the blind man to him. The text reads: "He ordered that he should be summoned," so that he might approach God and eternal light. Psalm 33:6 states: "Come to him and be enlightened, and your faces will not be ashamed." Genesis 44:21 has: "Bring him here to me, and I will set my eyes on him."

Third is that at Christ's order the blind man is summoned: "And they summoned him," the ministers of enlightenment and the intercessors, "and said to him," to the blind man who was on the brink of being immediately enlightened. 2 Corinthians 2:8 says: "Assure him of your love for him."

"Take courage." Tobit 5:13 has: "Be of good courage, your cure from God is imminent." Baruch 4:5, 4 states: "Be courageous, O people of God, since the things that are pleasing to God have been made known to us."

So "Get up," that is, raise yourself up for the light of heaven. Ephesians 5:14 says: "Rise up, sleeper, and arise from the dead, and Christ will enlighten you."

"He is calling you." Romans 4:17 reads: "Who calls things that are not as though they were."

Fourth is the hastening of the blind man to the light as "he throws off his garment," so that he might show reverence and throw off the behavior of his former error through confession. *The Song of Songs* 5:3 states: "I have put off my garment. How will I put it on?" Ephesians 4:22 says: "You are to put off your former behavior and the old human being, which is being corrupted through deceptive lusts."

"He sprang," out of the joy and hope he had in being cured. *The Song of Songs* 2:8 has: "Behold, he comes, leaping upon the mountains, skipping over the hills," since even if he were lame, he would have leapt for joy. And this was a sign of perfect faith, for otherwise he would not have conceived of such joy. Isaiah 35:6 says: "Then will the lame leap as a hart, and the tongue of the dumb will be opened."

"He came to him," the Savior and Illuminator of all. 1 Samuel 25:8 states: "We have come to you on a good day."

"And Jesus answered and said to him." In this fifth point the Lord, through a question, wants to show affection to others like this blind man: "What do you want me to do for you?" He asks this not because he doesn't know the answer, but so that it might be shown to others that his desire is not just for something physical, but to be able to see internally and externally. Tobit 5:12 says: "What joy will I have who used to sit in darkness and did not see the light of heaven?"

"But the blind man said to him," exclaiming his desire to see the light. Qoheleth 11:7 states: "The light is sweet, and it is delightful for my eyes to see the sun." "Rabboni," my sweet master, who enlighten all with your truth, who said in John 8:12: "I am the light of the world. The person who follows me does not walk in darkness, but will have the light of life." Further on, in John 9:39, you said: "I have come into the world for judgment so that those who do not see may see and that those who see may become blind." "That I may see." Luke 18:41 reads: "Lord, that I may see." Psalm 17:29 states: "My God, enlighten my darkness."

"But Jesus said to him," Jesus, who is the fountain of true light. Wisdom 7:26 says: "[You are] the brightness of eternal light and the unspotted mirror [of God's majesty]." "Go on your way," with perfect enlightenment. This is the sixth observation. Psalm 88:16-17 states: "Lord, they will walk in the light of your countenance, and in your name they will rejoice all day long. And in your justice they will be exalted." Baruch 3:14 says: "Learn where the light of the eyes is and where peace resides." "Your faith," by which you believe that I can do this for you, "has saved you." Luke 7:50 reads: "Your faith has saved you. Go in peace."

"And immediately he began to see." This is the seventh consideration. "Immediately," since the grace of the Holy Spirit does not drag out the cure. And lest one think that he was healed by medicine, the miracle happened immediately, in an instant. Thus, he saw *tout de suite*. Psalm 118:18 states: "Open my eyes, and I will consider the wondrous things of your law." Acts 9:18 has: "There fell from his eyes something like scales, and he recovered his sight." Micah 7:8 reads: "When I sit in darkness, the Lord is my light."

"And followed him on the way." The fruit of the miracle is its utility. Matthew 8:19 says: "I will follow you wherever you go," since he was finally following light and didn't want to return to darkness. John 12:36 says: "While you have light, believe in the light that you may be children of the light." Ephesians 5:8 reads: "Walk as children of the light." For the primary benefit of light is that we follow the light.

SCRIPTURE

LUKE

JOHN

ACTS OF THE APOSTLES

ROMANS

1 CORINTHIANS

2 CORINTHIANS

GALATIANS

NON-BIBLICAL SOURCES